TO MARTIN

HAPPY CHRISTMAS

LOVE

John

DECEMBER '85.

Dear Popsy: Collected Postcards of a Private Schoolboy to his Father

Dear Popsy

Collected Postcards of a
Private Schoolboy to his Father

by

E. BISHOP-POTTER
With Illustrations by Paul Cox

ANDRE DEUTSCH

To
Jason, hero and friend

With special thanks to
R. Keen, J. Marley
and C. Dyter for their help
and encouragement

First published 1984 by
André Deutsch Limited
105 Great Russell Street, London WC1

Phototypeset by Falcon Graphic Art Ltd
Wallington, Surrey
Printed in Great Britain by
Ebenezer Baylis & Son Ltd
The Trinity Press, Worcester and London

ISBN 0 233 97692 2

St Cloud's

Dear Popsy,

Arrived 6 p.m. after a beastly train journey (I was pinched all the way by a frightful old man in a Harris tweed jacket). As for St Cloud's, it's awful – gargoyles everywhere and each one looking like Great Aunt Amethyst without her spectacles. I hate it here.

Basil

P.S. Please forward my saffron pyjamas.

St Cloud's

Dear Popsy,

No, I have not settled in. I will NEVER settle in. Why did you send me to this beastly place? There must be nicer schools I could have gone to. I wish I was dead.

Basil

P.S. Where are my saffron pyjamas?

St Cloud's

Dear Popsy,

I feel bleak, BLEAK! Everything here is horrid. Even the trees are the wrong shape. If I must stay, then send me chintz and a few bits of Mother's jade to brighten my room. Send too the bronze of St Alice.

Basil

P.S. WHERE ARE MY SAFFRON PYJAMAS?!!

St Cloud's

Dear Popsy,

If you don't send my saffron pyjamas I shall scream!

Basil

P.S. This evening at supper I was smiled at by a boy wearing scarlet nail polish!

St Cloud's

Dear Popsy,

I have chummed up with the boy with the nail polish. His name is Gemini Tarqqogan (yes, two q's, though he spells it with three!). After lessons we take tiny walks through the grounds of St Agnes the Divine's – a filthy nearby church where each morning at seven (seven, would you believe!) we attend Thanksgiving Service.

Basil

St Cloud's

Dear Popsy,

Thank you for your 'Saturday' letter. Yes, I too enjoy Saturdays. They're such heavenly fun.

I can't wait for you to meet my friend Gemini – he's so decadent. Yesterday at Mass he wore three violets – at his knee! Honestly, I've never known anyone quite like him.

Basil

P.S. Gemini sometimes wears a frock!

6

St Cloud's

Dear Popsy,

What a peach you are for sending so much fudge. I shared it with my friend Gemini and another boy called Courtney Durham (he's awfully odd) and we were all quite sick. The food here is horrid. This morning I found a reddish hair in my porridge.

Basil

P.S. Gemini thinks my saffron pyjamas the end. Has St Alice been sent under separate cover?
P.P.S. I simply loathe rugby.

St Cloud's

Dear Popsy,

Will you please tell Mother to stop writing. I'm quite tired of hearing about her beastly varicose veins. I sometimes wish they'd burst. St Alice arrived this morning. She's such a comfort.

Basil

P.S. At rugger practice (ugh!) this afternoon my friend Gemini called the coach – Rory O'Brien – a silly old queen and was given 100 lines – 'I must not use slang'!
P.P.S. Gemini says that Rory O'Brien is madly keen on Courtney Durham, the boy I shared my fudge with.

St Cloud's

Dear Popsy,

You ask for information on Gemini. I knew you would! Well, he has the curliest dark hair and the longest fingers (he says they're made for flower arranging, and I quite believe him) that I have ever seen. You'd adore him. Last night he made me swear on the bible that I'd never grow my nails longer than his!

Basil

P.S. Mother is still writing.

Dear Popsy,

Yes, I do have fagging duties. My 'Lord and Master' is a chap called Hugo Bletchworth who spends most of his time at the local abbatoir and who sometimes visits a psychiatrist. I have been ordered to his (Bletchworth's) rooms tomorrow evening for sherry. Gemini was a bit put out when I told him.

Basil

P.S. Bletchworth has the most extraordinary collection of leather things.

St Cloud's

Dear Popsy,

I don't care that Mother's varicose veins are worse. I DON'T CARE!

Basil

P.S. My sherry evening with Bletchworth was too odd. After drinks he gave me something to smoke and I dropped off. When I woke half my clothes were missing and he was thrashing me with a strip of dried goat meat! Honestly, this school!

St Cloud's

Dear Popsy,

    URGENT!!! Gemini is having a fancy dress party on the 25th and I haven't a thing to wear. Gemini is going as Salome and says I would make a perfect Nubian slave. Please, please hunt out a scrap of loincloth (leopard skin would be nice) from the attic and forward it post haste.

Basil

P.S. Rory O'Brien, the rugger coach, is going to the party too – as Queen Victoria!

St Cloud's

Dear Popsy,

    Gemini thinks you too scrumptious (I've told him *every-thing* about you!) and invites you to his fancy dress party. Gemini says that if you do come, don't wear a wedding gown. Courtney Durham (Rory O'Brien's protégé) will be going as Miss Havisham and we can't have *two* brides.

Basil

P.S. I'm rather worried about the loincloth. Where is it?
P.P.S. This afternoon I was thrashed by Bletchworth who wore nothing but a leather apron!

St Cloud's

Dear Popsy,

    Thank you for your letter and the money. What a peach you are. Gemini's fancy dress party was too screamy. Halfway through the evening Bletchworth turned up absolutely blotto and practically dragged me from Gemini's arms. As for Rory O'Brien, he was in hysterics – somebody trod on his tiara and bent it!

Basil

P.S. The loincloth was exactly right. I'm sure I should feel quite at home in a jungle!

9

St Cloud's

Dear Popsy,

I'm in a spot of trouble. One of the tutors spied us leaving Gemini's party (Courtney Durham was practically naked!) and has reported us to the Head. There's going to be an awful fuss.

Basil

St Cloud's

Dear Popsy,

I have to tell you that the Head intends writing you about Gemini's party. He thinks our behaviour 'a scandal' and has confined us (Gemini, Courtney Durham and myself) to our rooms. Gemini was given an extra punishment – 1,000 lines – for making a face and wearing mascara!

Basil

P.S. This morning Bletchworth gave me a thrashing for no reason at all. I didn't mind a bit!

St Cloud's

Dear Popsy,

I don't care what the Head says, I was not covered in rouge. I may have had on a smear or two but nothing more. The old goat is obviously confusing me with Gemini who wore heaps. Well, he *was* Salome.

Basil

P.S. I had a dreadful time at confession this evening!

St Cloud's

Dear Popsy,

Did you know that your writer friend, Inigo Frick, is up this way? I saw him yesterday in a tea shop. He was wearing a lilac suit and carried a matching umbrella. He asked me to send you his *love*!

Basil

P.S. A thrashing tonight from Bletchworth – the fifth in three days!

10

St Cloud's

Dear Popsy,

I have seen a delicious rosary with a silver fingers-entwined clasp (I think they're fingers!) which I simply must have. Do be a peachypoos and send me five pounds so that I may buy it.

Basil

P.S. No, I've no idea where Inigo Frick is staying.

St Cloud's

Dear Popsy,

Thank you for the five pounds. The rosary really is the dearest of things. My Father Confessor, Father Absolute, has seen it and says that if it wasn't for the fact that he is short of 'readies' he would get one for himself. You'd adore Father Absolute; he's such a wheeze and as common as muck. Yesterday entering St Agnes the Divine's he rinsed his false teeth in the font! Gemini says he (Father A) swears like a trooper and drinks Communion wine by the bucketful!

Basil

P.S. I'll do my best to locate Inigo Frick.

St Cloud's

Dear Popsy,

My face looks awful today. There is a pimple on my left cheek and one on the right. No news of Inigo Frick. I saw a flash of lilac along the High Street on Wednesday but it turned out to be Mrs Maharaj, the school cook. I will continue to make enquiries and will write you as soon as I have any information.

Basil

P.S. Courtney Durham's mother seethes. The Head has written to her over Gemini's fancy dress party and she threatens to remove Courtney to another school. Rory O'Brien, poor dear, is inconsolable. At rugger practice this afternoon I'm sure I saw a tear!

St Cloud's

Dear Popsy,

Thank you for your letter which made me giggle ever so much. What heavenly fun you have. The only news this end is that Courtney Durham has been reprieved. His mother is allowing him to stay on provided he is chaperoned by 'that nice boy Bletchworth'! Rory O'Brien is over the moon.

Basil

P.S. Tonight Bletchworth thrashed me with my rosary – on the altar in St Agnes the Divine's!

St Cloud's

Dear Popsy,

It makes me unhappy to know that you are not eating. Do try to eat something – even if it's only a little cake.

Popsy, the strangest thing has happened. The thrashing Bletchworth gave me with my rosary has produced an immense bruise (you'll never guess where!) which bears a perfect likeness to St Lucy of Syracuse. I intend showing it to Father Absolute.   Basil

St Cloud's

Dear Popsy,

Thank you for the parcel. You're a perfect peach. How wonderful that your appetite has returned. Here's more tasty news! Father Absolute is convinced my bruise is a Sign! Yesterday he spent half an hour examining it (quite closely!) and afterwards lit two candles. He now intends writing to the Pope (or The Missus, as he calls him) about it.

Basil

St Cloud's

Dear Popsy,

I'm having the most awful trouble with my bowels. Will you please send the enema thing that mother uses.

Basil

P.S. I think I have discovered where Inigo Frick is staying.

St Cloud's

Dear Popsy,
    Thank you for the enema apparatus (what a dreadful noise it makes!). Inigo Frick is staying at a Carthusian monastery – the Order of St Orville's (Gemini calls it St Awful's!) – two miles from here. I shall try to visit him next week and give him your note.

Basil

P.S. Father Absolute wants to photograph my bruise!

St Cloud's

Dear Popsy,
    I have visited Inigo Frick at the monastery – an awful place full of stale bread crusts. Inigo became quite helpless when I gave him your note and had to rest in a confessional box. What *have* you two been up to?! He vows to write soon.

Basil

P.S. Mother's enema has caused the most immense stir here. Everyone wants one! Gemini has suggested that we hold an Enema Evening and is frantically searching for something in magenta tubing!

St Cloud's

Dear Popsy,
    You make the dinner party sound dreadful. I'm sure it couldn't have been – not if Uncle Herbert was there. He's such a scream.
    Father Absolute is positively besotted with my bruise. For the past week he's done nothing but point his Leica at it! Gemini hates him and threatens to write something vile on the back of his surplice!

Basil

P.S. Is Uncle Henry really dying?

13

St Cloud's

Dear Popsy,

Gloriana! Father Absolute has framed a photograph of my bruise and it now stands alongside a dish of sacramental wafers in St Agnes the Divine's. At communion on Friday he couldn't take his eyes off it!

Basil

St Cloud's

Dear Popsy,

Inigo Frick popped in yesterday and took me to lunch. We had heaps of gin! He told me he is leaving the monastery and returning to London. Does this mean that you are 'chums' again?

Basil

P.S. Bletchworth whispered to me today that he would like to thrash me to death!

St Cloud's

Dear Popsy,

Thrilling news! Father Absolute plans a special service in St Agnes the Divine's on Sunday to commemorate my bruise! Heavens, I feel almost saintly!

Basil

St Cloud's

Dear Popsy,

Your letter was a treasure and did me the world of good. The Service of the Bruise was too perfect for words. Simply everyone turned up. Gemini made a frightfully rude noise during the Magnificat but apart from that everything was terribly religious. Father Absolute was positively reckless with the Holy Water! He said afterwards that it was 'the best do' he'd ever officiated at!

Basil

St Cloud's

Dear Popsy,

Everyone, but EVERYONE, wants to see my bruise. It's quite made me famous! Bletchworth has insisted that I charge a viewing fee and has taught me to waggle certain muscles so that St Lucy's nose moves. Thus far we have collected £5!

Basil

P.S. If Mother worships me as you say she does, why doesn't she send me money? However, I promise to write her soon.

St Cloud's

Dear Popsy,

Gemini has invited me to spend a weekend at his mother's country home – The Clowts. He says the gardeners there are divine! I have written Mother today.

Basil

P.S. Bletchworth is terrified that my bruise will fade and keeps painting it with indelible pencil. Yesterday a 'customer' said it looked like Wallace Beery! Life is one long waggle!

St Cloud's

Dear Popsy,

I really can't understand why Mother was so upset by my letter. I thought I was too sweet for words. Why is she so gruesome?

Basil

P.S. Mother seems to have forgotten to send the lace bits I asked for. Would you be a dear and remind her of them.

St Cloud's

Dear Popsy,

How awful about Uncle Henry passing on. Did he leave me anything?

Basil

15

St Cloud's

Dear Popsy,

Dear, adorable Uncle Henry. £10,000 – *and* his monocle! If he were alive I'd almost hug him! Please send the cheque quickly. I really don't want his beastly old monocle so perhaps you will give it to one of the servants. Would cook like to have it, do you think?

Basil

P.S. Bletchworth is thrashing away like mad – last night with Mother's enema tube!

St Cloud's

Dear Popsy,

I throb for the cheque – where is it? Bletchworth is planning a lavish inheritance party and we simply MUST HAVE MONEY!

Basil

P.S. Gemini and I are off to The Clowts this weekend.

St Cloud's

Dear Popsy,

Cheque safely to hand. So many noughts! I felt quite giddy looking at them! My stay at The Clowts was a dream – huge gardeners everywhere and all reeking of geraniums. Gemini's mother is divine. She has a perfectly wicked dalmatian called Harry Boy who is fed on artichoke omelettes and who follows her everywhere. They look at each other in the most extraordinary way!

Basil

St Cloud's

Dear Popsy,

Well, if you will go out in the pouring rain without proper clothing you must expect a chill. Anyway, I do hope you are now in good health. My inheritance party was a scream. We

16

held it in the back room of the Last Faerie – an inn in town. Father Absolute came along and did the sauciest things with his prayer beads! Write to me soon.

Basil

St Cloud's

Dear Popsy,

I have bought a racehorse!

Basil

St Cloud's

Dear Popsy,

Don't be beastly about the horse. You'd worship it if you were to see it – such heavenly hocks! Bletchworth got it for me for a song – eight thousand guineas. We're having it trained by Inky Pryce whose handling of geldings is the talk of the Turf. His jockey, Nipper Thompson, is practically a midget, but ever so sweet. He has a little hump.

Basil

P.S. What racing colours should I choose? Gemini says Nipper Thompson would look perfect in baby pink!

St Cloud's

Dear Popsy,

We are to name the horse The Bruise – after you know what! Father Absolute, bless his chasuble, suggested The Bruise Adored but Bletchworth thought it a bit much.

Basil

P.S. I hope you are not determined to be beastly about my horse.

P.P.S. Bletchworth dragged me from my bed last night and gave me the most heavenly thrashing.

17

Dear Popsy,

Sorry if my calling you beastly upset you, but it did rather seem from the tone of your letter, Popsy dear, that you didn't approve of The Bruise. So glad you do now. Next to Gemini I don't think I've ever seen anything quite so scrumptious. Yes, I have settled on my racing colours. The sleeves will be of the palest lavender and the tunic the colour of Cezanne's apples (or are they tangerines?). When I told Inky Pryce he said something terribly blunt!   Basil

St Cloud's

Dear Popsy,

Having a lovely time spending Uncle Henry's money. Yesterday I bought Bletchworth a pair of jackboots and a bullwhip, and Father Absolute a giant jigsaw puzzle of the Last Supper (he's having the most awful trouble finding the loaves!) Courtney Durham and Rory O'Brien have asked for something for their 'bottom drawer'!

Basil

P.S. Mother writes that she and Aunt Amethyst are off to Rome. What a vile place to visit. Gemini says that once you've seen one Michelangelo you've seen the lot!

St Cloud's

Dear Popsy,

You'll be thrilled to fragments to hear that you have been made an honorary member of a club which Gemini and I have just formed – The Brides of St Cloud's. We meet in the back-room of the Last Faerie. Father Absolute is chairman and Bletchworth treasurer. Rory O'Brien and Courtney Durham are also members. Bletchworth asks you to send your membership fee of five guineas.

Basil

P.S. You'd adore the Last Faerie. It's managed by a blond young man called Maurice Le Vere who was once something with Sadler's Wells. He calls Father Absolute 'Mother'!

St Cloud's

Dear Popsy,

Thank you for your membership fee. You are now a Bride of St Cloud's.

Basil

P.S. The Bruise has been entered for a five-furlong race at Newbury next month. Father Absolute prays every night that it will win and has sent my jockey, Nipper Thompson, a lucky crucifix.

St Cloud's

Dear Popsy,

Just back from a trip with the Brides to Inky Pryce's stables – a divine day among the tack. Inky introduced us to his wife who wore something grey and smelled horribly of horse rub! Gemini had to turn his head away! The Bruise is too masculine for words. What a size! Stubbs would have swooned!

Basil

P.S. Nipper Thompson hates my colours and says he'd much rather be seen in heliotrope!

St Cloud's

Dear Popsy,

I have mumps, but don't worry, I'm not in any pain – well, just a little. I must have caught them during my visit to Inky Pryce. We did spend quite a lot of time with the stable lads and I do recall giving one of them (he had the vaguest eyes!) a sip of gin from my hip flask. Everyone here is perfectly sweet to me. Gemini has filled my room with lilies and visits me every day, as does Courtney Durham. I spend the time painting my toenails!

Basil

St Cloud's

Dear Popsy,

Thank you for the tiny 'get well' card. The verse is too ghastly, but I adore the boy with the conkers – such a leer he has! Inky Pryce telephoned on Tuesday and was perfectly beastly. He blames me for giving mumps to his stable lads!

Basil

P.S. Aren't you being rather naughty asking Inigo Frick to stay with you while Mother is away?

St Cloud's

Dear Popsy,

Wondrously well again and prettier than ever! Gemini says the mumps have done miracles for me! Tonight we (the Brides) celebrate my recovery with a party at the Last Faerie. Father Absolute promises a surprise!

Basil

P.S. (Midnight) A shuddersome time at the LF. One simply couldn't move for gin! Half way through the evening Maurice Le Vere changed into a tutu and feathers and danced a pas de deux with Father Absolute! Aren't they the utter end!

St Cloud's

Dear Popsy,

Thrilling news from Inky Pryce. The darling Bruise is to run in the last race at Newbury on Saturday. You've no idea how excited everyone is. The Brides are quite in a flutter. When I told Courtney Durham he was sick in Rory O'Brien's lap! Do keep your fingers crossed.

Basil

Dear Popsy,

Wasn't it too horrid of The Bruise? Last of 15! I could have died. Bletchworth was absolutely furioso. He accused Nipper Thompson of being drunk in the saddle and had to be prevented from thrashing him (he carries his bullwhip everywhere!). I must say, Nipper did seem to teeter rather when he left the scales. We all feel quite ruined.

Basil

P.S. Gemini lost an eyelash in a bowl of lobster soup and was in a ghastly mood all day. The only time he smiled was when the King's horse slipped up!

P.P.S. My colours looked heavenly.

St Cloud's

Dear Popsy,

Sorry to hear that you lost heaps on The Bruise. Didn't we all, duckie! Father Absolute's Restoration Fund for St Agnes the Divine's is positively devastated!

Basil

P.S. Gemini has bought himself a blonde wig and a chemise!

St Cloud's

Dear Popsy,

Thank you for the dear things you say. I miss you too. Nipper Thompson called in yesterday to apologise for his riding of The Bruise. He seemed quite upset, poor luv. As a penance Gemini made him bare his hump and then drew the most hideous face on it . . . in eyebrow pencil (Louisa Fryman's Archly Through The Night). Later we all went to the Last Faerie where Bletchworth got terribly pickled and tried to set fire to Maurice Le Vere's cat! Isn't he a panic.

Basil

St Cloud's

Dear Popsy,

Inky Pryce tells me that The Bruise is 'coughing fit to bust' and will not run for at least another two months. Isn't it too ghastly. I would rush to him if I thought it would do any good, but he probably wouldn't even recognise me. I have told Inky that no expense must be spared in getting him back his health and that he is to inform me immediately there is any change in his condition. Have I done the right thing? I do hope so.

Basil

P.S. We have a mystery. Bletchworth has suddenly taken to disappearing after lights out. The whole school is in a fever over it. This morning he returned carrying a huge parcel tied with black satin ribbon!

P.P.S. Do you think I'd look well in vermillion?

Dear Popsy,

Wouldn't you simply know it . . . Mother writes from Venice complaining about her beastly varicose veins. She says that once in Rome she plans to have His Holiness lay a hand on them. Heavens, who'd be the Pope!

Basil

P.S. Apparently Aunt Amethyst has had a 'dreadful experience' with a gondolier – lucky old thing!
P.P.S. Bletchworth continues his nightly jaunts and is simply rolling in money.

St Cloud's

Dear Popsy,

Your soirée sounds a perfect scream. One can just see Inigo in Mother's nightdress and feather boa. How Beardsleyan! Gemini is terribly upset that you didn't invite him. He's dying to try out his blonde wig!

Basil

P.S. Bletchworth turned up at the Last Faerie tonight in a new knee-length leather coat covered in metal studs! With his bullwhip and jackboots he looked quite heroic.

St Cloud's

Dear Popsy,

You haven't forgotten that it's my birthday next week? I'd adore something in Indian musoree silk.

Basil

P.S. Gemini has just walked into my room wearing earrings!

St Cloud's

Dear Popsy,

Bless you for the dreamy bed sheets. Such a heavenly black. I/we feel too utterly decadent between them! No gift from Mother yet. How I loathe her.

Basil

P.S. My birthday gifts from the Brides were an opium pipe and Montesquieu's *Persian Letters*. As a special treat Father Absolute allowed me to listen in on the Head's confession. Aren't they pets.

St Cloud's

Dear Popsy,

Such excitement! We've discovered what Bletchworth has been up to on his nightly flits. Gemini (he can be so determined when he wants to) followed him to an hotel and saw him leave with (you'll never guess) . . . Courtney Durham's mother! Gemini said she had a huge lump of sticking plaster on her back and looked quite contused! When we told Courtney he tittered!

Basil

P.S. My birthday present from Mother arrived this morning . . . a revolting pair of rugger boots. I've given them away.

St Cloud's

Dear Popsy,

Gemini asks if you'd be a dream of a dream and seek out a caftan and gold sandals (size six) from Harrods. We're having an awful end-of-term dance on Friday week and he's going in 'disguise'! He insists that the caftan be of magenta hue.

Basil

P.S. Gemini wants me to spend my holidays with him at The Clowts. Please say that I may.

24

St Cloud's

Dear Popsy,
    Gemini adores you and says that your taste is too perfect. The caftan and sandals are exactly what he wanted. He can't wait for the school dance. I am to be his escort for the evening!
                                                              Basil
P.S. Courtney Durham's mother is in a private nursing home suffering from nervous debility and severe lacerations to her back! Bletchworth has been asked by her doctor not to visit her!

St Cloud's

Dear Popsy,
    A perfectly magic evening at the end-of-term dance. Gemini's disguise fooled everyone and he was quite the prettiest thing there. How his sandals shone! The Latin prof danced with him six times, though I had the Last Waltz. Rory O'Brien said we made the perfect couple!
                                                              Basil
P.S. Off to The Clowts tomorrow.
P.P.S. I'm afraid my school reports are simply ghastly!

The Clowts

Dear Popsy,
    Having a divinely gritty time among the potting sheds. The gardeners seem bigger than ever!
                                                              Basil
P.S. Gemini's mother has taken to playing hymns on an accordion. Her Te Deums are out of this world!

The Clowts

Dear Popsy,

How I wish you were here with us. How you'd love it. It's such fun, though not without a little pain! This morning the head gardener chased me into a thicket of hawthorn and I am now in bed with my thighs in shreds. Gemini's mother has ordered a young servant called Billy to dust them (my thighs!) with lavender talc every half hour. Bliss!

Basil

P.S. Doesn't this heat make you feel too depraved?

The Clowts

Dear Popsy,

Thank you for being such a sweetie about my school reports. Aren't they awful! I'm told that my Latin/Greek marks are the lowest ever recorded. Still, who cares about silly old Socrates!

Basil

The Clowts

Dear Popsy,

Guess who has turned up here . . . Hugo Bletchworth and Courtney Durham's mother! They arrived unannounced on Saturday from a yachting holiday in Villefranche. She absolutely adores the boy and calls him 'My Liege'! They spent the whole of Sunday polishing his jackboots – she sitting at his feet on an inflated air cushion!

Basil

P.S. A servant has just asked me if I heard screams coming from Mrs D's bedroom last night!

The Clowts

Dear Popsy,

Gemini and I return to St Cloud's on Sunday. You've simply no idea how madly melancholic we both are. If it weren't for the Brides being there I'm sure we'd go quite to bits.

Basil

P.S. Bletchworth came down to breakfast this morning wearing a leather cuirass!
P.P.S. Gemini's mother plays the accordion night and day. I've hardly had a wink of sleep.

St Cloud's

Dear Popsy,

Back at beastly St Cloud's and feeling too wretched for words. I have scribbled a poem called The Clowts Divine which I shall send to Gemini's mother together with a box of chocolates. Do write to me.

Basil

St Cloud's

Dear Popsy,

Your letter cheered me up no end. Now for more cheer. Nipper Thompson called in today with the news that The Bruise is fully recovered and will run at Sandown on the 27th. Be sure to put some money on him. Nipper says he will 'go like the wind'.

Basil

P.S. I think Nipper is dyeing his hair!

St Cloud's

Dear Popsy,

Mother writes from Florence asking for news of my school progress. I've written back saying that everyone is thrilled to pieces with me, so should she ask you please be a dream and say the same. Must dash, Gemini has an appointment with a dressmaker and he wants me to help him choose material. Basil

St Cloud's

Dear Popsy,

Thank you for your letter of commiseration. Wasn't it too gruesome of The Bruise – last again, and favourite too. I can still hear the boos. Nipper Thompson hasn't stopped crying for a week. Gemini is the only one who isn't upset. He backed the winner – simply because the jockey's colours were the same as his frock – burnt sienna and gold! Basil

St Cloud's

Dear Popsy,

Here is a funny story. Our house tutor called us to his rooms today and asked if there were any subjects we would care to specialise in. Courtney Durham said he wanted to take a course in mothercraft and was given 1,000 lines! Isn't he a scream. Basil

28

P.S. Nipper Thompson says Inky Pryce is to enter The Bruise for a mile race, poor thing.

P.P.S. Nipper's becoming awfully outré. He now speaks with a lisp and his hair is the colour of cheese custard! Gemini has given him the name of his dressmaker!

St Cloud's

Dear Popsy,

How ghastly about Inigo Frick. Liverpool Street Station! Heavens, what a place to be arrested! Which court does he appear at and when? Do telegraph more details. What is the 'serious offence' he is charged with?

Basil

P.S. Gemini says he wouldn't be seen dead at Liverpool Street Station.

St Cloud's

Dear Popsy,

Thank you for your telegram. The Brides are quite determined to attend Inigo's hearing. Do you think he'll mind? We'll be having breakfast at Claridge's and Gemini has suggested we pay the quickest visit to Harrods before going on to Bow Street. It will be heaven to see you again.

Basil

St Cloud's

Dear Popsy,

The Brides have asked me to thank you for giving them such a divine day. Gemini says you are almost too cuddlesome! So glad you liked him. Isn't he criminally pretty. I must say, Inigo didn't seem the least put out when the magistrate called him those revolting names. I would have swooned! We've still no idea where Rory O'Brien and Courtney Durham slipped off to.

Basil

P.S. Father Absolute apologises for his behaviour and vows never to touch another drop.

St Cloud's

Dear Popsy,

I have had two letters from Mother this week both concerning her varicose veins. Honestly, Popsy, she's quite driving me insane. You must tell her to stop writing. Nipper Thompson telephoned today asking if he might add a ruche or two to my colours. Isn't he a dear. Father Absolute implores that we make him an honorary member of the Brides.

Basil

St Cloud's

Dear Popsy,

I have started shaving! Gemini too – his face *and* legs!

Basil

P.S. Courtney Durham's mother has bought Bletchworth a wolfhound which he keeps in one of the cellars here.

P.P.S. Dear Nipper Thompson is to be an honorary member of the Brides. A special ceremony conducted by Father Absolute is to be held in the Last Faerie on Monday. Nipper was quite overcome when we told him. He said that next to winning the Derby he couldn't imagine anything more thrilling!

St Cloud's

Dear Popsy,

Today (Friday) the English prof found a letter (a terribly amorous one!) that I wrote Gemini. I have been reported to the Head and appear before him on Monday. I expect he will make a frightful fuss, the old tart.

Basil

P.S. Monday. The Head was vile about the letter and has stopped my cocoa for a week. I loathe him.

P.P.S. Gemini has been given 500 lines for plucking his eyebrows during Thanksgiving Service!

30

St Cloud's

Dear Popsy,

I think I'm going to shriek. Mother plans to visit me here as soon as she returns from abroad. You must put her off. I simply couldn't stand a day of varicose veins.

Basil

P.S. Gemini and I have discovered the most heavenly game to play. If I tell you it involves transparent oilskins and raspberry jam. . .!

St Cloud's

Dear Popsy,

Mother is due here on the 28th. If you cannot put her off do insist that she wears surgical bandages.

Basil

P.S. Bletchworth's dog escaped last night and practically devoured the gatekeeper!

St Cloud's

Dear Popsy,

I will meet Mother's train only if she wears surgical bandages.

Basil

P.S. I'm simply covered in raspberry jam!

St Cloud's

Dear Popsy,

Mother was too gruesome for words. She said vile things about my room and spoke of Gemini as 'that little madam'. I've quite made up my mind never to see her again.

Basil

P.S. Her surgical bandages were the most dreadful colour.
P.P.S. Gemini has been chosen to play Ophelia in the school's production of *Hamlet*. He's too insane with joy and quite determined to make the Old Vic sit up!

31

Dear Popsy,

I should positively loathe a day at the zoo. Do suggest somewhere a little more chic – like Cartiers. Gemini says the lighting there does wonders for one!

Basil

P.S. Have you tried Louisa Fryman's newest mascara – Noir Pour Moi? It's simply made for Ascot.

P.P.S. Gemini has quite been taken over by Ophelia. He does nothing but look derelict.

St Cloud's

Dear Popsy,

I did write – last week – but I lost the card. One of these days I'll lose my head, I know I will. A frantic Guy Fawkes party at the Last Faerie on Friday. Simply everything went wrong. Gemini laddered his stockings and the fire brigade had to be called out after Bletchworth threw a lighted banger in the rum punch! Poor Maurice Le Vere's sitting room is burned to a frazzle! I do hope you are keeping well.

Basil

St Cloud's

Dear Popsy,

Inky Pryce telephoned today insisting that The Bruise be gelded. I won't allow it, I won't!

Basil

P.S. It took me two hours to do my hair today – TWO HOURS! I sometimes wonder whether it's worth the effort.

P.P.S. Courtney Durham's mother has bought Bletchworth a bronze of Our Lady of Pain!

St Cloud's

Dear Popsy,

Criminally happy! The school magazine is to publish a poem I have written! It's called 'P.S. to Proust' and begins: 'Does Albertine leave brilliantine upon your silken pillow?' I shall send you a copy as soon as it appears in print.

Basil

32

Dear Popsy,

So glad you're glad about the poem. Is it naughty? Madly! I'm sure if Proust were here to read it he'd giggle like anything. Gemini says I should have titled it 'You can't have your Madeleine and Eat It'!

Basil

P.S. Courtney Durham and Rory O'Brien have been seen doing the most extraordinary things in the gymnasium!
P.P.S. Gemini is having his dressmaker design him a complete wardrobe for Ophelia. For the death scene he has ordered something in hand-printed silk chiffon!

St Cloud's

Dear Popsy,

Mother asks for the return of her enema apparatus. I really can't bring myself to write to the old thing so will you please tell her that I have mislaid it. (I think Father Absolute may have borrowed it to spray the bluebottles in St Agnes the Divine's!)

Basil

St Cloud's

Dear Popsy,

Are you really having the poem framed? How wonderful. Do hang it in the library – near the classics.

Basil

P.S. Gemini makes his stage debut on the 15th. We're having the most enormous party afterwards.
P.P.S. Bletchworth's dog is keeping the whole school awake with its howling.

Dear Popsy,

Do we have to spend Christmas at Grandmother Castleton's – you know how she reeks. I'm sure it was Mother's vile idea. Do try to dissuade her.

Basil

P.S. Gemini had a dress rehearsal yesterday and got into the most awful trouble for carrying a handbag. He told the drama master he didn't feel dressed without one!

St Cloud's

Dear Popsy,

What a night you missed! Gemini's Ophelia was too screamy! Heavens, the rouge he wore, and how he undulated! In Act III he called Hamlet 'dearie'! The whole cast is absolutely livid with him.

Basil

P.S. Have you talked Mother out of spending Christmas at Grandmother Castleton's? I simply couldn't bear it.

St Cloud's

Dear Popsy,

    Mother can insist all she likes – I am not spending Christmas at Grandmother Castleton's, so there.

Basil

The Grand

Dear Popsy,

    Where do you think I am? Brighton! Yes, Brighton! It's awful! The wind! I'm with Father Absolute and Nipper Thompson. We do nothing but comb our hair and drink gin! Merry Christmas!

Basil

The Royal

Dear Popsy,

    Now in the above after being ejected (quite vigorously!) from The Grand. Apparently Nipper Thompson was discovered in Father Absolute's room wearing green silk stockings (green!). The linen maid screamed when she saw him. Happy New Year!

Basil

P.S. Isn't this weather too shiversome?

The Royal

Dear Popsy,

    Where is my Christmas present, but where? I simply ache for it. So pleased you liked my little gift. I was going to get a darker colour but Gemini thought lemon would suit you better. He's ever so clever with colours.

Basil

P.S. Father Absolute was sick at the dinner table this evening and had to be helped to his room.

Dear Popsy,

A Japanese screen! How madly divine! I simply wept when I saw it. The colour is perfect – and those wicked little wrestlers. . .! I could look at them all day! The Brides are quite salad-like with envy.

Basil

P.S. Guess what Mother bought me . . . A chemistry set! I had someone blow it up.

P.P.S. Courtney Durham is wearing a diamond engagement ring!

Dear Popsy,

Not you too! It's awful isn't it. I haven't stopped sneezing for a week. Gemini won't let me near him! Do keep warm.

Basil

P.S. This morning Gemini was sent from the history class for suggesting that Madame Du Barry was a new brand of face cream!

P.P.S. I've just sneezed again!

Dear Popsy,

Beastly news. First The Bruise has injured a fetlock in training and won't be fit for the start of next season, and second Inky Pryce says that unless he (The Bruise) is gelded it is unlikely that he will ever win a race. What *am* I to do? The idea of the poor luv being snipped at is too mortifying. I sometimes think the whole world is against me, I really do.

Basil

St Cloud's

Dear Popsy,
     You're quite right of course. It would be heavenly to see
my colours in the winners' enclosure. It's just that I hate to
think of The Bruise as being incomplete. No matter, I shall
instruct Inky to cut!

Basil

P.S. Yesterday Bletchworth killed a stray cat with his bullwhip! That boy!

St Cloud's

Dear Popsy,
     I can hardly scrawl. The school's heating system has
broken down and we are all simply freezing to death. Do send
heaps of hot water bottles as soon as possible.

Basil

St Cloud's

Dear Popsy,
     I purr like a kitten cat in from the cold. The hot water
bottles have quite saved my life. How could I manage without
you? So glad you are feeling better, I'm still blowing like mad.

Basil

St Cloud's

Dear Popsy,
     Off to Inky Pryce's with the Brides on Saturday to see the
knife put to The Bruise's belongings. Isn't it too exciting. I'm
simply dying to see them close up!

Basil

P.S. Gemini is being fitted for a corselet!

St Cloud's

Dear Popsy,

A perfectly thrilling day at Inky Pryce's. The Bruise was too heroic – not a murmur – though he did give me the oddest look as the knife went in! After surgery Inky's wife (Gemini said she looked as though she had just run a two-mile race and finished second) gave us lunch – rabbit stew and dumplings! Father Absolute made the sign of the Cross over them!

Basil

P.S. Courtney Durham seemed terribly interested in the operation!

St Cloud's

Dear Popsy,

Do not worry about me. My cold has quite gone and I am as fit as anything. I can't imagine why you should think I would enjoy Emily Brontë. All those dreary old moors and things. Ugh!

What a dear Nipper Thompson is. You simply won't believe it but he has sent me a pickle jar containing the Bruise's off-comings! I've stood them alongside my bronze of St Alice.

Basil

St Cloud's

Dear Popsy,

I don't wish to know that Mother's veins are swelling terribly. For all I care they can be the size of hawsers. Do find something interesting to write about.

Basil

P.S. I caught a glimpse of Bletchworth's dog this evening. It was too hideous for words. Half its hair has gone and one of its eyes is missing!

38

St Cloud's

Dear Popsy,

I'm in the most beastly hole. The Head popped into St Agnes the Divine's late tonight and found Gemini and I au naturel (I adore French don't you?) and raspberry jammed! Heavens, what a sight we must have looked! Anyway, the vile old beast has suspended us and intends writing you. Do be a dear and calm him down.

Basil

P.S. I'm sure I saw a crocus this morning.

St Cloud's

Dear Popsy,

Your letter made me die. Did the Head really call us depraved?! What an old ruin he is. Anyone would think it was his raspberry jam! Thanks ever so for smoothing things over. (Smoothing things over! Jam!)

Basil

P.S. Gemini collected his corselet today. It is lilac with the tiniest black stitches.

St Cloud's

Dear Popsy,

And about time too! Haven't I always said that Mother should have the veins removed – HAVEN'T I? When will she be admitted to the clinic?

Basil

P.S. How heroic of Mother to have Sir William perform the operation. Wasn't it he who ruined Uncle Freddie's hernia?

St Cloud's

Dear Popsy,

Don't you think it time that Sir William hung up his scalpel? First Uncle Freddie's hernia, now Mother's varicose veins. Thank heavens you didn't send me to him for my you-know-what operation!

Basil

P.S. Gangrene is quite serious, isn't it?

St Cloud's

Dear Popsy,

I know it was too terrible of me but I couldn't help a titter when I read of Mother's amputation. Will she have to wear one of those hideous false legs that creak all the time? How awful for you.

Basil

P.S. Gemini had his hair permed today!

St Cloud's

Dear Popsy,

Please don't ask me to visit Mother at the clinic. I know I'd be ill if I were to see her leg. Ugh!

Basil

P.S. Guess who I saw reeling from Bletchworth's rooms last night, her wrists tied with lighting flex and her Brussels lace in tatters? . . . Mrs Durham! Isn't it too odd.

St Cloud's

Dear Popsy,

Of course we should sympathize with Mother. It must be beastly having only one-and-a-quarter legs (how could one skip or anything?) but no, I will not visit her. I've told you, Popsy Mopsy, I couldn't bear to see her S-T-U-M-P.

Basil

P.S. Last night Gemini and I got raspberry jammed to Beethoven's Ninth. You should have seen me during the *allegro energico*!

St Cloud's

Dear Popsy,

Mother writes that she intends convalescing at Grandmother Castleton's and would like me to spend a few days with her. She wants me near her, she says. Oh Popsy, do get me out of it.

Basil

P.S. The school governors visit here tomorrow so today has been spent tidying up. Courtney Durham was given some embroidery to repair!

P.P.S. Has Mother had her false leg fitted yet? Gemini says that if he had to wear a false leg he'd have it wallpapered!

St Cloud's

Dear Popsy,

You simply must be the dreamiest peach ever and rescue your boysie. The beastly English prof has given me 1,000 lines – 'I must not flaunt my hips in front of the school governors' – and wants them a.m. Monday. The thing is, Popsypoos, I'm weekending with the Brides at Hastings so won't have time to write them. Will you be a dear and write them for me? Be sure to complete them by tomorrow (Saturday) and send them special delivery. Ta ever so. Basil

St Cloud's

Dear Popsy,

What an old silly you are! You needn't have written the lines! No, it was a joke! I wasn't given any lines. Heavens, what a goose; they must have taken you hours! The Brides have been in hysterics about it. We didn't for a moment think that you would do them.

Basil

P.S. Last night Gemini slept with two orchids in his armpits!

St Cloud's

Dear Popsy,

How was I to know that you had a business appointment? If I'd known I wouldn't have asked you to write the lines, would I? Really, if you can't take a joke. . .

Basil

P.S. I don't care that Mother is wearing her false leg. I hope it gets wet and rusts.

41

St Cloud's

Dear Popsy,

Yes, I was put out by your letter. You were perfectly beastly to me. However, I will forgive you if you help pay The Bruise's training bill. It's heaps – £250.

Basil

P.S. Nipper Thompson has had his ears pierced!

St Cloud's

Dear Popsy,

You angel cake, you. I really didn't expect you to pay the whole £250 but now that you have I could hug you to shreds.

Basil

P.S. A ravishing time at the Last Faerie last night. The gin! Nipper Thompson wore pearl-drop earrings!

St Cloud's

Dear Popsy,

Your night out with Mother sounds utterly awful. Heavens, what a thing to have happened. Surely Mother must have realised that the leg was loose. Weren't you frightfully embarrassed? I would have died. I am writing a new poem 'Memo to Montesquieu'. I'm sure I'd look delicious in a garret!

Basil

P.S. The Head saw Nipper Thompson and Father Absolute yesterday walking arm-in-arm along the High Street – Nipper wearing black organdie and a hat with cherries on it! Father A told the Head that Nipper was his niece up for the day to visit him. What a scream!

St Cloud's

Dear Popsy,

    I knew it, I simply knew it! I said to Gemini only the other day, I'll bet you anything you like Mother writes to me complaining of her false leg – and she has. This morning I received a letter saying that she's having trouble with the joints. Really, Popsy, her varicose veins were bad enough but if she's going to go on and on about a beastly tin leg I don't know what I shall do. I'm sure Sarah Bernhardt's family never had this trouble.

Basil

P.S. Gemini and Nipper Thompson insist that I have an auburn rinse. Do you think I dare?

St Cloud's

Dear Popsy,

    Too late . . . I'm now most awfully auburn!

Basil

St Cloud's

Dear Popsy,

    The Bruise runs on Saturday and Nipper Thompson says to put our shirts on him. The price, he thinks, will be heaps to one.

Basil

St Cloud's

Dear Popsy,

    I'm so livid I could stamp. Why does The Bruise do this to me? Heavens, Mother could have run faster! Did you lose heaps? We did. Father Absolute says he will have to start selling his Holy Nails again!

Basil

St Cloud's

Dear Popsy,

But I am being patient. Goodness, how long must I wait before I see my colours cheered? It wouldn't be so bad if The Bruise were to come second or third, but to be last all the time. . . It's just too much. Bletchworth says that if The Bruise were his he'd put the whip to him. By the bye, Bletchworth has now taken to marching up and down the quad and insisting that the first years salute him!

Basil

St Cloud's

Dear Popsy,

I've swapped The Bruise for a chaise longue. I visited Inky Pryce and there it was (the chaise longue) standing in the scullery. Well, I simply fell in love with it. Inky says I've got a bargain. Apparently it went right through the French Revolution and was once owned by a senior jockey club steward who shot and ate his Derby runner after it broke down in training.

Basil

P.S. The chaise longue has the dreamiest little legs with baby toes on them. Courtney Durham is to knit bootees for it.

St Cloud's

Dear Popsy,

You may think me wrong but Gemini says I am right. Gemini says The Bruise has no more chance of winning a race than Father Absolute has of getting into a Junior Miss girdle!

Basil

St Cloud's

Dear Popsy,

I languish like a trollop! My chaise longue arrived today and I simply can't tear myself from it. I adore it. Tomorrow I will get nectarines to nibble as I loll.

Basil

P.S. Enclosed is a photograph which Gemini and I had taken at Hastings last weekend. The two dreamy things with us are fishermen. Aren't they huge? The one with his arm around Gemini has a tattoo in the most extraordinary place!

St Cloud's

Dear Popsy,

I too had a heavenly Sunday. Courtney Durham's mother turned up and invited us to lunch. The food! Clotted cream, wild strawberries, cold turkey and ham; simply everything. Mrs Durham couldn't eat any of it because her face was in bandages. When Gemini asked her what the trouble was she just looked at Bletchworth and smiled!

Basil

St Cloud's

Dear Popsy,

We have a beauty in the family – me! I have just been voted Miss Cup Cake of St Cloud's! Isn't it a scream. The whole thing was Gemini's idea. We were having drinks at the Last Faerie when out of the blue he suggested a contest to find the prettiest Bride. (I'm sure he only suggested it because he was wearing a new frock and thought he would win). Anyway, Courtney Durham, Nipper Thompson, Gemini and myself paraded before the rest of the Brides and I was judged the winner. Gemini was furious and practically snapped Nipper Thompson's head off when Nipper asked him to dance. My prize was a 10-oz tub of Louisa Fryman's Wrinkle Vanish!

Basil

St Cloud's

Dear Popsy,

But I thought I'd told you . . . I shall be holidaying with Gemini at The Clowts. You don't mind do you? Oh, those gardeners!
Basil

St Cloud's

Dear Popsy,

I suppose I could spend a few days with you, but only if you promise to take me somewhere dreamy. No beastly zoos or museums or anything.

Basil

P.S. You're quite sure Mother will be at Grandmother Castleton's?

St Cloud's

Dear Popsy,

I shall be on the 2 o'clock train arriving Victoria at 3.45. Be sure to meet me. Look for a boy with auburn hair and a bangle on his wrist! I'm dying to see you again.

Basil

P.S. Gemini asks you not to keep me too long!

The Clowts

Dear Popsy,

I write this in a potting shed. The sun is shining on my hair and standing quite close to me is a rugged little gardener called Albert who yesterday allowed me to trim his moustache with a pair of secateurs. I've never been so happy.

Basil

P.S. Thank you for a dreamy three days.

The Clowts

Dear Popsy,

Weather too vile to go out so my morning was spent winding wool for Gemini's mother who is knitting her dog Harry Boy a winter coat. Tonight Gemini and I are to meet two gardeners for gin.

Basil

46

The Clowts

Dear Popsy,

Just back from a boating trip on the lake with Gemini and Albert the gardener – me reading aloud from *La Vie de Bohème* and Gemini painting his nails under a rosy parasol. Monet to a T! Basil

The Clowts

Dear Popsy,

A chase in the woods today with Albert the gardener rampant in pursuit. I let him catch me twice. How his moustache tickles! Do take care, and write to me.

Basil

P.S. The cook here has reported that three jars of raspberry jam have gone missing!

Dear Popsy,

Off this afternoon for a peek at a nearby ruin. Apparently he adores young boys and for a peck on the cheek will allow you to inspect his Beardsley prints – the naughty ones!

Basil

P.S. Gemini has just ticked off one of the maids for dropping his hairnet in the marmalade!

Dear Popsy,

Gin on the lawn today and later Confession. How I lied! I'm told the priests here can't keep their mouths shut.

Basil

Dear Popsy,

The whole day spent under a pear tree making daisy chains and writing our names over and over on lavender paper. Heaven. Tonight we bathe in the lake with the wondrous Albert.

Basil

P.S. A postcard this morning from Courtney Durham and Rory O'Brien who are camping in the Cairngorms. They say it's freezing there but they are having a lovely time keeping each other warm!

Dear Popsy,

Just back from Mass; too yawnsome for words. (Why is the Elevation of the Host always such a let down?) We return to St Cloud's on Friday. Albert says he's going to miss me 'something rotten'!

Basil

48

Dear Popsy,

I simply gush with news! First, Courtney Durham's mother is again in a nursing home – a victim of Bletchworth's passion, it is thought – and second, Inky Pryce has sacked Nipper Thompson for wearing earrings at morning gallops! Nipper is now staying with Maurice Le Vere at the Last Faerie where he does nothing but drink green chartreuse. He's awfully upset, poor dear.   Basil

St Cloud's

Dear Popsy,

Gemini and Courtney Durham yesterday visited Courtney's mother in the nursing home. She's quite unable to speak and has to be fed through a tube, poor thing. Gemini says she looks as though she's been hit by Harrods!   Basil

St Cloud's

Dear Popsy,

Your note made me giggle so much that I dropped a great blob of Louisa Fryman's Wrinkle Vanish on my chaise longue. Serves Inigo right. Doesn't he know that hod carriers hate to be called dearie – well, most of them! I do hope your back is better.

Basil

P.S. Whatever you do don't buy any of Louisa Fryman's Wrinkle Vanish. It's turned my chaise longue green!
P.P.S. I've sent some (Wrinkle Vanish) to Mother!

St Cloud's

Dear Popsy,

The Bruise ran at Sandown today and won at 20-1. I'm so upset I cannot write more.

Basil

P.S. If you say I told you so I shall scream and scream.

St Cloud's

Dear Popsy,

Your letter didn't help a bit. Of course I know there are not many boys of my age who have their own chaise longue, but what has that to do with anything? I've been made the laughing stock of the whole school. Gemini says I should return the chaise longue to Inky Pryce and insist that he gives me back The Bruise. I shall do as he suggests.

Basil

St Cloud's

Dear Popsy,

Inky Pryce says he has no intention of returning The Bruise. The exchange, he says, was made in the presence of witnesses and anyway the chaise longue has been ruined by Louisa Fryman's Wrinkle Vanish. I could kill him.

Basil

St Cloud's

Dear Popsy,

There's no need to feel sorry for me, really there's not. I no longer care about The Bruise. Good riddance to it. I still have Gemini and the Brides. Gemini's been such a comfort. He says he'd much rather be with me on a chaise longue than ruining his stockings in some muddy winners' enclosure.

Basil

P.S. Mother has written me complaining that the Louisa Fryman Wrinkle Vanish has brought her out in a rash!

St Cloud's

Dear Popsy,

This evening the Brides collected Mrs Durham from the nursing home, then went to the Last Faerie for a coming out party. Bletchworth was there in his leather and looked quite crocodilean. How he creaked! Mrs D gave a little whimper when she saw him! To mark the occasion Maurice Le Vere concocted a drink especially for the Brides. It's called A Girl's Best Friend and consists of three parts tequila, two parts vodka and two parts cider. Father Absolute drank ten and tore off Nipper Thompson's skirt! Basil

St Cloud's

Dear Popsy,
So glad you made heaps on the shares. You are a clever old thing. Nothing is happening here. Courtney Durham has bought himself a sewing machine but that's about the only news worth telling. Isn't life a yawny old yawn?
Basil
P.S. I wrote the above last night. Since then Courtney Durham has run up two pyjama tops for Rory O'Brien and a blouse for Nipper Thompson!

St Cloud's

Dear Popsy,
Bletchworth will be in Harley Street on Thursday to see a specialist. Can you put him up for the night? I have told him that you will. Be sure to keep the cats away from him.
Basil

St Cloud's

Dear Popsy,
A. I never knew Mother had a spare leg.
B. What was it doing on the staircase?
C. I'm sure Bletchworth only meant to put a little dent in it.
D. Where did he get the hammer?
E. Have you counted the cats?
Basil

St Cloud's

Dear Popsy,

Mother has written to the Head complaining of Bletchworth's attack on her spare leg. Why is she so vile? Bletchworth says he has no recollection of the incident.

Basil

P.S. Courtney Durham is machining away like mad. The noise!

St Cloud's

Dear Popsy,

If Mother is ordering another spare leg and having the ruined one repaired that will mean that she will have three false legs! Heavens, Popsy, you soon won't be able to move for the beastly things.

Basil

P.S. Gemini says that to have three false legs is vulgar.

St Cloud's

Dear Popsy,

Ta ever so for the cherry pie. I ate it on my chaise longue and flicked the stones at Gemini. You should have heard him shriek! We had a paper chase today and I fell into a ditch and quite hurt my leg. If there's one thing I hate it's a paper chase.

Basil

P.S. At Thanksgiving Service this morning I saw Father Absolute wipe his nose with the Humeral Veil!

St Cloud's

Dear Popsy,

Will you please be a dream and send me one of Mother's spare legs. Don't say no. Gemini's made a hanging basket from an old copper kettle and I simply must get one over on him. If you don't send the leg by return of post I will never speak to you again.

Basil

52

Dear Popsy,

Leg safely to hand! I was too terrified to touch it at first but plucked up courage and took it to a blacksmith who for four shillings punched holes in it and painted it a heavenly sage green. It now hangs from my ceiling with trailing ivy at the knee and dreamy blue lobelia peeping from the ankle. Tomorrow I shall buy a scarlet geranium to stick in the top. It's quite the talk of the school!

Basil

P.S. The most frightful howling sounds have been coming from Bletchworth's rooms tonight.

St Cloud's

Dear Popsy,

Don't worry. If Mother makes a fuss about the leg tell her that one of the servants stole it. But listen do, I have news; the severed head of Bletchworth's dog has been found floating in the font of St Agnes the Divine's! It bobbed up during Low Mass yesterday and almost scared a first year to death. Isn't it too eeksome. Father Absolute has reported that he heard something go plop the previous night but thought it was a late penitent blowing bubble gum! The Head has ordered an inquiry.

Basil

St Cloud's

Dear Popsy,

No, I will not return the leg. I would have nowhere to put my lobelia. Why didn't you do as I suggested and tell Mother one of the servants had stolen it?

Basil

P.S. Even if I were to return it it would be of no use to Mother. There's a drainage hole where the big toe should be and heaps of other holes for flower arrangement.

St Cloud's

Dear Popsy,

I need your help. Mother writes that if I don't return the leg she will come to the school and take it by force. You must stop her, Popsy. I'd die of shame if I were to see her stomping along the quad. Promise her another leg – a pretty gold one, anything.

Basil

St Cloud's

Dear Popsy,

Isn't Mother being rather greedy asking for two legs? However, if it will keep her away from here then please be a peachypoo and buy them for her.

Basil

St Cloud's

Dear Popsy,

You needn't have bothered to tell me about The Bruise, Nipper Thompson had already done so. I suppose you backed it and won heaps.

Basil

St Cloud's

Dear Popsy,
No, your letter didn't upset me. If you must know I've been too ill with toothache to write but I'm sure you won't want to know about that.

Basil

St Cloud's

Dear Popsy,
Thank you for the money – it's quite made my toothache disappear!

Basil

St Cloud's

Dear Popsy,
A one-day holiday on Friday so Gemini and I are popping over to Paris for the weekend. Quelle fun!

Basil
P.S. Gemini's teaching me the French for 'May I meet your brother/father/uncle'!

Hotel de Savoie

Dear Popsy,
Oo-la-la. Here we are in Paris! It's divine – not a bit French! Yesterday we visited the Louvre and saw the Mona Lisa. Gemini said she reminded him of his mother's chiropodist during bunion treatment! Au revoir.

Basil
P.S. Tonight we take absinthe with a brutish old onion seller and his friend.

55

St Cloud's

Dear Popsy,

Your letter was waiting for me when I returned. How brave you are. Have you told Mother yet? She'll scream when you do; you know how she loathes Inigo. Where will you live? Do find somewhere utterly chic and set aside a little room for me.   Basil

St Cloud's

Dear Popsy,

Chelsea! How romantic! I can just see you amongst all those palettes and things. Is it heaven and outré? How sweet of you to have taken my poem with you. I will visit you soon and bring something for your dear little kitchen.

                                             Basil

P.S. Please don't hang the poem in the kitchen. The steam might get under the glass and turn it brown.
P.P.S. Gemini asks if Inigo snores!!

St Cloud's

Dear Popsy,

A letter from Mother this morning. How she seethes! She calls Inigo an animal and says I must neither see nor contact you. I have written back saying I will see my popsypie whenever I please!

                                             Basil

P.S. I have bought you an embroidered 'Home Sweet Home' for your parlour and Courtney Durham has run up some gingham curtains for the kitchen.

St Cloud's

Dear Popsy,

I write this at midnight tormented by toothache. Oh Popsy, you've simply no idea of the agony I'm in. My face is swollen and I look too awful for words. I just want to die.

                                             Basil

St Cloud's

Dear Popsy,
     I'm tortured with toothache and all you can write about is
your vile kitchen and Inigo's beastly soufflés. I think I hate
you almost as much as I hate Mother.
                                                            Basil

St Cloud's

Dear Popsy,
     Please forgive me for being so beastly. Your note of the
25th reached me before the one of the 23rd and when I saw no
mention of my toothache I became quite angry. I knew in my
heart that you cared.
                                                            Basil
P.S. I will be in London on the 7th to see your pretty new
house.
P.P.S. Thank you for the tincture. It's so soothing, and in
such a dear little bottle too.

St Cloud's

Dear Popsy,
     I've told the Brides all about No.38 and they simply can't
wait to see it for themselves. You should have heard Courtney
Durham sigh when I mentioned the duchess satin bedsheets.
He's ever so thrilled at your liking his curtains.
                                                            Basil
P.S. Feeling too heroic after having my tooth filled. I didn't
scream once. The dentist said I had the prettiest gums he'd
ever seen. His were awful.

St Cloud's

Dear Popsy,

The Head called me to his study today and told me that Mother had instructed him to give me two days leave of absence. A car is to collect and take me to Grandmother Castleton's (ugh!) tomorrow. I'll bet you anything you like Mother wants to talk to me about you and Inigo. I dread going.

Basil

P.S. The Head asked me if there were any problems at home so I simply had to tell him that you had left Mother to set up home with a man. He made the most awful face!

St Cloud's

Dear Popsy,

Mother says you are a disgusting pervert and that she will never see you again. Honestly Popsy, she simply L-O-A-T-H-E-S you. She also says she now regards me as the head of the family and as such I must start behaving like a man! When she said that I began to giggle like anything and she flew into the most terrible rage. She says you're to blame for my 'inadequacy'! She hates you, she really does.

Basil

P.S. Her leg!

St Cloud's

Dear Popsy,

There's really no need to explain to me why you left Mother, I quite understand. Heavens, I'm sure if I were in your place I would have left the beastly old tart ages ago.

Basil

58

St Cloud's

Dear Popsy,

I haven't stopped crying for two whole days. My room
was ragged on Monday and everything quite ruined. Mother's
leg was flattened and one of The Bruise's off-comings nailed to
the wall. Aren't some people beasts. Bletchworth has promised to investigate.

Basil

P.S. Bletchworth has started calling me Corporal!

St Cloud's

Dear Popsy,

Your letter with its funny stories quite cheered me up.
Now, here's a funny story to cheer you. Yesterday the art
tutor set us an essay to write on the Cubists. Gemini wrote one
line . . . 'If only they drew circles. . .'! Doesn't he make you
die.

Basil

P.S. One of the boys who ragged my room has met with the
most dreadful accident – two broken arms and a broken leg.
Nobody knows how it happened and the boy is refusing to say.
Bletchworth suggests that he may have been thrown from a
window!
P.P.S. The red stain is raspberry jam!

St Cloud's

Dear Popsy,

Maurice Le Vere needs your help. One of the local
magistrates, Sir Geoffrey Grassington, is threatening to close
down the Last Faerie. Apparently he looked in on Monday
and found Nipper Thompson quite naked doing a fan dance!
Maurice asks if you know Sir G and if so, whether you could
contact him and calm him down. Do help if you can.

Basil

Dear Popsy,

How should *I* know if Sir Geoffrey is one of the Uxbridge Grassingtons? You'll have to write to him and find out, but do hurry – poor Maurice is quite distraught.

Basil

P.S. Nipper Thompson has been evicted from the Last Faerie and is now sleeping under the altar in St Agnes the Divine's. Father Absolute has had to ask him not to keep his make-up in the monstrance!

St Cloud's

Dear Popsy,

Father Absolute tells me that Sir Geoffrey *is* an Uxbridge Grassington. Does that mean you know him? Can you black-mail him or anything? DO ACT QUICKLY!

Basil

St Cloud's

Dear Popsy,

Goodness knows what you wrote to Sir Geoffrey but Maurice Le Vere says that he (Sir G) is now behaving like a perfect luv. It seems he called into the Last Faerie today and bought everyone a drink!

Basil

St Cloud's

Dear Popsy,

The most awful news . . . Courtney Durham's mother has been found dead in a ditch two miles from the school. Police say she was murdered! Isn't it ghastly. The Head has told us that detectives will be here tomorrow to speak to us. Bletchworth says that if I am asked what I was doing on the evening of the 14th I'm to say that I was playing Ludo with him.

Basil

P.S. Courtney Durham had to identify the body and took his crochet along! He said it was in shreds – the body.

St Cloud's

Dear Popsy,
    Bletchworth has been charged with Mrs Durham's murder! He appeared at court this morning and was remanded in custody for a week. I wasn't there, but I'm told B was dressed from head to toe in leather and before being taken to the cells saluted the magistrates! The Brides have ordered him some chocolate éclairs from Harrods.

Basil

St Cloud's

Dear Popsy,
    Mrs Durham's funeral was held on Tuesday. Courtney wanted all the Brides to be there but the Head allowed only Courtney and Rory O'Brien to attend. Rory afterwards told us that on the way to the church Courtney stopped off at a drapers and bought six yards of curtain material!

Basil

St Cloud's

Dear Popsy,
    Bletchworth is to stand trial at Lewes Assizes. What beastly luck; I'm sure he'd have much preferred the Old Bailey. The police have taken statements from the Brides and have told us that we may have to appear as witnesses. Isn't it a thrill. Gemini is already preparing his outfit.

Basil

P.S. Courtney Durham has been told that he is the sole beneficiary of his mother's will. He'll come into heaps.

61

St Cloud's

Dear Popsy,

A letter this morning from Bletchworth in H.M. Prison Strangeways. How brave he is; hardly a word of complaint – just a little grouse about the warders. He says they're all cissies and need a good dose of discipline. I am sorry to hear about your back. Do take care of yourself.

Basil

P.S. Bletchworth is sharing a cell with a Mr Harold Gabbage who poisoned his wife and three children. It's so nice to know he's not alone.

P.P.S. An auburn rinse last night. I think I overdid it!

St Cloud's

Dear Popsy,

I have written to Bletchworth and passed on your message. I'm sure he will appreciate it. As cook says, every little helps. The Head called us to his study today and lectured us on how he expected us to behave in court. Gemini was wearing rouge and was told to wash it off. I was asked if I had spilled iodine on my hair!

Basil

St Cloud's

Dear Popsy,

Bletchworth's trial starts on Monday. We were told only this morning (Saturday) so you can imagine the panic we are in. There's so much to do. Gemini and I have spent the whole day trying to decide which clothes to take. We travel tomorrow to Lewes where rooms have been reserved for us at the Railway Hotel.

Basil

The Railway Hotel

Dear Popsy,

Arrived 9 p.m. tired out, and with Gemini seething. The Head saw us off and when he spotted Gemini's hat boxes (there were heaps of them!) he made him open all his luggage. Well, it was simply full of frocks and things! The Head ordered him to replace them with 'more suitable clothing'! Gemini was furious and hasn't spoken a word since. I don't think he's going to make a very good witness!

Basil

The Railway Hotel

Dear Popsy,

Courtney Durham gave evidence today. Honestly, what a scream! Every time he was asked a question he started to giggle. In the end the judge became so cross that he threatened to put Courtney in the cells until he composed himself. Well, after that, Courtney just went to pieces and had to be given water which he couldn't drink because it wasn't Perrier! Rory O'Brien is furious with the judge.

Basil

P.S. Gemini and I give evidence tomorrow, Friday. Be sure to cut out all the newspaper reports.
P.P.S. Father Absolute hasn't been sober since we arrived.

The Railway Hotel

Dear Popsy,

Just back from court! What a thrill! I was in the witness box for only five minutes but I wouldn't have missed it for the world. How the heads turned when I walked into the court-room! I simply blushed like anything. Poor Bletchworth, though, I think his dear mind has gone. As I was taking the oath he shouted, 'Slope arms'! It was all too embarrassing. He did the same when Gemini gave evidence. Heavens, Gemini! He absolutely slithered into the courtroom – and the mascara!

Basil

The Railway Hotel

Dear Popsy,

Guilty but insane. Isn't it too ghastly. The Brides were quite overcome when the verdict was announced (Courtney Durham let out a cry). We understand that Bletchworth is to be sent to Longmoor Asylum. Gemini says that in Longmoor itself there's a heavenly little restaurant which serves the most delicious madeira cake.

Basil

St Cloud's

Dear Popsy,

Got back yesterday to find Bletchworth's rooms ransacked by souvenir hunters. What beasts. I have had to pay five shillings to a horrid third year for a pair of Bletchworth's old shoes. Heaven alone knows what they'll want for his bullwhip. After supper the Brides went to the Last Faerie where we drank a toast to B and sang his favourite song – 'Boiled Beef and Carrots'. Everyone was in floods.

Basil

P.S. Sir Geoffrey Grassington was at the Last Faerie. What an odd fish. Those scary eyebrows, and how he ogles one!

St Cloud's

Dear Popsy,

Thank you for the newspaper clippings. Gemini says we should paste them into a pretty scrapbook and send them to Bletchworth at Longmoor. Isn't it a perfect idea. We are also writing to the governor asking when we may visit.

Basil

P.S. I quite agree with Inigo about Correggio's cherubs. Gemini does too. Gemini says they remind him of Walls' pork sausages!

Dear Popsy,

I simply drooled when I saw the cake. If you keep sending me such yummy things I'll never get into my clothes! Tonight the Brides met to discuss Mrs Durham's monument. Courtney said she was rather keen on elephants and suggested a pair of crossed tusks. Gemini said that if *his* mother was fond of elephants she'd have a whole herd! Nipper Thompson said that when he dies he'd like as his monument a huge replica of Louisa Fryman's Kissable Lipstick! What a scream! Nipper suggested that Mrs D's inscription read 'One of the Best'!

Basil

St Cloud's

Dear Popsy,

Two letters today – one from Mother saying vile things about you and Inigo and the other from the governor of Longmoor Asylum stating that Bletchworth will not be allowed visitors for at least eight weeks. Such a long time to have to wait before we see the boy. I think of him all the time.

Basil

St Cloud's

Dear Popsy,

Thank you for the money. Your trip sounds dreamy. How I envy you. It's not fair that I have to stay here and do beastly schoolwork while you have lovely fun all the time. Don't do too much walking, you know how your feet swell.

Basil

P.S. The gatekeeper told me this evening that a man in a string vest was asking for me!

St Cloud's

Dear Popsy,

Sorry to hear about your ankles, but I did warn you not to do too much walking, didn't I? You have only yourself to blame. Gemini suggests you abandon the high heels for a while and the swelling will go down! Isn't he terrible.

Basil

St Cloud's

Dear Popsy,

I heard today that dear Mr Gabbage – the mass poisoner who shared Bletchworth's cell – has also been found insane and is to be sent to Longmoor. Isn't it too wonderful. He'll be such a comfort to poor B. I have written to the governor asking that they be allowed to take tea together. I do hope he says yes.

Basil

St Cloud's

Dear Popsy,

I knew you'd be pleased for B. As you say, everyone needs a friendly face to turn to in times of trouble. No word yet from the governor. Perhaps he is too busy to write. The poor luv must be rushed off his feet with all those patients to care for. Talking of feet, so glad to hear that yours are better.

Basil

St Cloud's

Dear Popsy,

A letter this morning from Longmoor's governor thanking me for my concern over Bletchworth and advising that as soon as Mr Gabbage has settled in he will arrange for the two to have tea together. Isn't he a peach. I shall write back telling him that Bletchworth's favourite sandwiches are cream cheese with a layer of thinly-sliced cucumber.

Basil

Dear Popsy,

Bletchworth has been poisoned! The beastly Mr Gabbage slipped deady nightshade into a cheese sandwich during their little tea party and B is now in Longmoor's medical wing with a serious stomach disorder. The news came this morning from Longmoor's guv. I can't help feeling that I am to blame. If only I hadn't suggested the meeting.

                                        Basil

P.S. I washed my hair this evening and I've never seen it look so silky.

Dear Popsy,

Yes, I suppose I am being silly. Nobody could possibly have guessed that Mr Gabbage would do such a thing. Longmoor's guv tells me he has given him a frightful ticking off and has instructed his gardeners to clear the grounds of deadly nightshade. Bletchworth, he says, is now fully recovered and is making cardboard boxes which the asylum sells to a soap factory. I think that's sweet, don't you?

                                        Basil

Dear Popsy,

Your offer is too tempting, but on that day I go with the Brides to inspect and advise on Mrs Durham's monument. Apparently the stonemason is having trouble keeping the tusks (yes, she is to have tusks) upright and wants a decision on whether or not he should sink them in concrete. Gemini is against the idea and suggests they be fixed to ebony models of elephant feet with space for bedding plants. I think that that would look rather odd, don't you? Do enjoy yourself.

                                        Basil

Dear Popsy,

I sometimes think I have a genius for a daddy. What a perfectly lovely idea. Suspended tusks! I've told Courtney Durham and he has instructed the stonemason to get working on them right away.

Basil

P.S. Sir Geoffrey Grassington was again at the Last Faerie last night. Nipper Thompson danced a foxtrot with him and called him an old tart to his face!

St Cloud's

Dear Popsy,

Heavens, you and your suspended tusks! Anyone would think that it was *your* monument! Well, I'm sorry Popsy but they're simply not on. Courtney Durham's stonemason says that in a high wind they could pose a threat to visiting mourners. He now proposes that a tusk be fixed to each side of a headstone to form an arch above it. How dreamy! Courtney Durham, however, is determined to have something suspended and has ordered a small marble tablet bearing the words 'One of the Best' to be hung from the point where the two tusks meet. Thank goodness it's all settled. I was awfully pickled last night.

Basil

68

Dear Popsy,

But I am studying. I read all the time. At the moment I am reading the dictionary (Gemini says it's too boring for words!) and I have just finished *101 Beauty Hints* by Louisa Fryman (she swears by turnip juice). After the dictionary I shall plunge into Rupert Brooke, so there!

Basil

P.S. Courtney Durham's stonemason says he can get hold of a life-size elephant (recumbent) in green marble which would be perfect for Mrs D's tomb. Courtney has told him to snap it up.

Dear Popsy,

Your days sound as yawnsome as mine. Why does nothing exciting ever happen to us? If only we could do something wonderful. I so want life to be lurid, don't you? Gemini was saying the other day that when he finishes school he's going on a tour of all the best fashion houses in Europe. How scrumptious that would be. Do write to me soon.

Basil

P.S. Did I say nothing exciting ever happens? Well, I was wrong. Something too utterly exciting happened to me tonight. I was picked up by a navvy!

Dear Popsy,

I am writing a poem (yes, another!) in praise of dear Bletchworth. Oh, I'm too excited over it. Gemini has seen it and says that once it is finished I must send it to *Private School Verse*. Do you think I dare? It begins, 'Ne'er a thrasher like Hugo B, Ne'er a lasher as good as he' and it goes on about flex and ropes and things. Oh, I do so want it to be published. Tell me I should send it to *PSV*. Encourage me, Popsy, do.

Basil

69

St Cloud's

Dear Popsy,

Your letter thrilled me to bits. I knew you would encourage me, I just knew you would. Oh Popsypoos, it must be heaven to be a poet and grow hair everywhere. No, I never did finish my last poem. I couldn't get anything to rhyme with Montesquieu.

Basil

P.S. The Latin prof stopped me in the quad today and asked me if I was the boy who made the curtains. He wanted Courtney Durham of course. Courtney's making curtains for everybody.

St Cloud's

Dear Popsy,

My heart trills. *Private School Verse* are to publish my poem. The editor says it is the 'finest panegyric on sado-masochism' that he's read since 'Tie the Knots Tighter', written by a fourth year St Cloud's boy 10 years ago. How peachy! Honestly, I'm so thrilled I could wriggle. The Brides celebrate tonight with buckets of gin.

Basil

P.S. Just think, if Bletchworth hadn't killed Mrs Durham my poem might never have been written. I owe him so much.

St Cloud's

Dear Popsy,

I could tell from your note that you are as thrilled by the poem as I am. Do have it framed and hung next to the one I wrote on Mr Proust. The Bletchworth poem is much longer so the frame will have to be quite large. Something in rosewood I think, don't you?

Basil

70

Dear Popsy,

The Brides visit Bletchworth on Sunday 28th. We're all terribly excited. Courtney Durham has embroidered my Bletchworth poem in coloured silks which we will take to him. How I wish you could see it. It quite puts Aunt Amethyst's antimacassars to shame. Across the top are tiny rosebuds and violets, while down either side curl two emerald bullwhips. It took Courtney ages to do and he's ever so proud of it. Rory O'Brien says it makes the Bayeux Tapestry look like a dish rag!   Basil

Dear Popsy,

Our trip to Longmoor was too depressing. We were taken to a therapy shed wherein sat Bletchworth unpicking raw meringo wool. His poor hands! We all practically wept when we saw him. How sad he looked. How alone. I wanted to go up and hug him but the governor advised against it. Afterwards we had tea and madeira cake in this little restaurant that Gemini knows.

Basil

P.S. We were shown Mr Gabbage who seemed to be searching a hedgerow for something!

P.P.S. The governor loved my Bletchworth poem and is to hang it in B's cell.

Dear Popsy,

Our travels never end. On Saturday we are off to St Mildred's cemetery for the 'unveiling' of Mrs Durham's elephant. Oh, heavens, it's going to be a scream, I know it is. Every time I think of it I start to giggle. All those tusks and things! Gemini said yesterday that he didn't know whether to wear his black taffeta or a safari suit!

Basil

St Cloud's

Dear Popsy,

Thank you for the Madonna (what huge hands she has). I have stood her on my night table where she can watch over me, though there will of course be times when her face will have to be turned to the wall! So glad that your hair is no longer falling out. What a worry it must have been. I'm sure that if my hair were to fall out I'd shriek like anything. Mrs Durham's elephant is divine – so shiny and big. It even has a howdah which Courtney's stonemason says can be used as a shelter on rainy days. Each of the Brides had a sit in it and thought it ever so comfy.

Basil

St Cloud's

Dear Popsy,

Don't be such a tease, whose party and where is it to be held? Will there be tinsel and gin? Will I be swept off my feet by some wild welder in thrilling boots? If the answers are yes, yes, yes, then I will fly to it on wings of crêpe de chinon!

Basil

P.S. Courtney Durham's stonemason tells him that visitors to St Mildred's graveyard are now referring to Mrs D as the elephant woman!

St Cloud's

Dear Popsy,

How vile – sherry with Inigo's mother and sister. No, Popsypoos, it simply isn't me. I like parties where one may dance to a primitive drum. (I sometimes think I'm part Basuto!) Yes, I agree with you about Dostoevsky – he is divine (I have read *The Idiot* and simply adored it. How one could hug Prince Myshkin) but if I were to read all the books you suggest I'd never get any ironing done. I shall take the quickest peek at *War and Peace*, but nothing else.

Basil

P.S. Mother has been told of a Swiss inventor who has patented an artificial leg made of rubber. She hobbles to Grenoble next week to inspect it.

St Cloud's

Dear Popsy,

You say you dislike having to be serious with me, but you are never anything else. Heavens Popsypie, a boy has got to have fun. I'd die if I didn't have fun. Gemini says that one's schooldays should be divinely happy and that time spent studying is time wasted. He says there is only one lesson to learn in one's youth and that is never to yawn in profile, so there.   Basil

St Cloud's

Dear Popsy,

Mother writes from Grenoble that she has inspected the rubber leg and is to finance its production! Popsy, we must stop her. I have written asking her to think again. You must do the same. She is staying at the Meisterhoff Hotel. Write now. Rubber legs! Oh Popsy, how could she?

Basil

St Cloud's

Dear Popsy,

Yes, Mother did mention the inventor's name but I have forgotten it. It was terribly long and had heaps of esses in it – something like Oosterstreisles. Oh Popsy, if Mother refuses to listen to us we must have her committed. Can we do that?

Basil

P.S. A letter from Mother has just been delivered. She says she is quite determined to go into the leg trade and that factory premises have already been found. Production will commence as soon as the necessary machinery is installed! I think I'm going to scream.

73

St Cloud's

Dear Popsy,
     What a perfect idea. I'm sure that if you were to visit
Mother at Grenoble she would change her mind. Tell her that
I am ill with worry and that as head of the family, as she said I
was after you left her for Inigo, I forbid her to continue with
this scheme and that she is to return home at once. Do write to
me as soon as you have spoken to her.
                                                  Basil
P.S. No, don't bring me back a cuckoo clock, I hate them.
Something in lace perhaps.

St Cloud's

Dear Popsy,
     So you approve of what Mother is doing. You approve of
her rubber legs. How could you! I don't care about profits,
only what people will think when they know we are involved
with surgical appliances. Perhaps we should urge Mother to
start manufacturing trusses and crutches and leg irons and
things. Go on, why don't you suggest it to her, WHY DON'T
YOU!
                                                  Basil

St Cloud's

Dear Popsy,
     Are you quite sure we will make heaps of money? Are you
quite sure our name will not appear above the factory gates?
How many shares will I have? Rubber legs, though! If only it
were something a little more chic.
                                                  Basil

St Cloud's

Dear Popsy,

Mother says there will be three major shareholders –
herself, Mr Oosterthing, the inventor, and me (you've been
left out!). Heavens, Popsy, I'm going to be rich! Isn't it too
divine. Mother says the company is to be called Limbrub Ltd
(how revolting) and that production is to start in 12 to 14
weeks. As soon as it does I am to be allowed to visit the factory
and see the leg for myself.

Basil

St Cloud's

Dear Popsy,

I'm so ashamed I could practically die. Yesterday in
Courtney Durham's room one of his beastly curtains customers asked if I were the heir to the rubber legs fortune. Oh
Popsy, you've simply no idea how I felt – how embarrassed I
was. How could he have known? I'm sure none of the Brides
would have told him. Has there been anything in the financial
or medical journals? I thought you said our name would not be
mentioned.

Basil

St Cloud's

Dear Popsy,

Can't you write to *The Times* denying our involvement in
Limbrub? How on earth did they find out? Do you think
Mother might have told them? It's just the sort of beastly
thing she would do. How I hate her. As for your question, am
I ashamed of being associated with a company that makes
artificial legs, the answer is yes. Yes, I am ashamed. Ashamed,
ashamed, ASHAMED!

Basil

P.S. Gemini says that Limbrub sounds like a lotion for
infected cattle, and he's right.

St Cloud's

Dear Popsypoos,

Do you really think we will be contributing to medical science? Do you honestly believe that? Oh, if only it were true! Pasteur, Curie, and . . .! How those darling amputees would love us! Do send me the article from *Medical World*. Revolutionary! Adjustable! Heavens!

Basil

St Cloud's

Dear Popsy,

Thank you for the clipping. I have shown it to the Brides who were thrilled to bits by it. Gemini says Limbrub Ltd will do for the limbless what Louisa Fryman has done for the lashless! Father Absolute, when profits were mentioned, said I was 'the luckiest little bleeder on God's dear earth'!

Basil

St Cloud's

Dear Popsy,

It seems I am unable to pick up a newspaper or magazine without reading about our rubber legs. They have quite made Mother and Mr Oosterthing famous. The *Catholic Engineer* says that amputees everywhere should get down on their knees and give thanks for them! Oh Popsy, to think I was once ashamed of being associated with Limbrub Ltd. Now I want the whole world to know – yes, the whole world!

Basil

P.S. I feel awfully Claridges today!

St Cloud's

Dear Popsy,

Mother writes that orders for the legs are pouring in from all over the globe (Tibet want six gross!). Isn't it too thrilling. Imagine, in a few months' time every dear little stump in the land will have a Limbrub Stroller (yes, that is to be the brand name) strapped to it. Oo, it just makes me want to squeal with pride.

Basil

P.S. Have you seen the picture of Mother in *Business Bulletin*? Doesn't she look ghastly.

St Cloud's

Dear Popsy,

Thank you for your letter and the money. What a dear you are. Yes, it is fortunate that mother got to Mr Oosterthing when she did. How awful if Ahab Supplies had beaten her to him. Did you know that Mother is to stay in Switzerland until production gets under way? She says the weather is ghastly and were it not for the Matterhorn she would quite go to bits.

Basil

St Cloud's

Dear Popsy,

The reason Mother doesn't answer your letters is because she hates you so. As for Inigo she would like to see him gutted (one of Father Absolute's words!). In her last letter Mother said that when you visited her she could hardly bear to speak to you and that she guessed the sole purpose of your visit was to secure a place on the Limbrub board. She said she would see you dead first!

Basil

St Cloud's

Dear Popsy,

Mother writes that the first of the machinery has been delivered and she is quite hopeful that production will commence next month. Factory and office staff are being interviewed and a general manager has been appointed. Isn't it too thrilling? Mother also reports the case of a French amputee who on waking from the operation called out for a Limbrub Stroller.

Basil

P.S. A visit to Mrs Durham's elephant on Sunday. We found a tin can in the howdah and 'Bert loves Cynthia' scratched on the trunk!

St Cloud's

Dear Popsy,

Mother and Mr Oosterthing are popping over to London for a few days next week and I am to have lunch with them. Mother says that if there is time Mr O will teach me to yodel!

Basil

P.S. Last week I wrote to Bletchworth telling him of the legs and promising him one filled with his favourite mint lumps. This morning I received a letter from Longmoor's governor saying that mint lumps are permissible but would I not send the leg as he feared it might be used as a weapon!

St Cloud's

Dear Popsy,

My lunch with Mother and Mr O was too ghastly. Mother wore that awful hat with the primrose plumes and spoke of nothing but the Matterhorn and my hair. As for Mr O, well I just wanted to hide. Can you imagine, yodelling in Claridges! Once, during soup, he tapped mother's tin leg with his spoon and said 'Zoon a robber von she vill haff'! I could have died.

Basil

St Cloud's

Dear Popsy,

Yes, you were mentioned but only in passing. Mother, when she was served her Gâteau Americaine, said it reminded her of your Bolonski – garish and rather improper. She then made noises about his Male Nude with Apples so for a joke I told her that you thought it had all the charm of sweetbreads à la Castillan. Well, with that she pushed away her Gâteau Americaine and said, 'I imagine he does'. And that was the only time you came up, Popsypoos. Sorry to hear about your tiff with Inigo.

Basil

Dear Popsy,

So happy I could twirl. Mother tells me that the price of a Limbrub share has simply soared. There's been nothing like it, she says, since Featherlite Protection. She also says that the Limbrub Stroller is expected to win the Design and Maintenance Golden Spanner Award! Heavens, I'm in a dream, I really am.

Basil

P.S. I've just twirled and smashed a plate!

Dear Popsy,

I shricked like anything when I read your letter. Why do you scare me so? Surely there will always be a demand for the Limbrub Stroller? People are having their dear legs off every day. Anyway, I'm quite sure our Mr O is inventing new things all the time. He's awfully clever you know. Mother says he can work miracles with a screwdriver.

Basil

Dear Popsy,

Mother says the future of Limbrub Ltd is no concern of yours, but if it worries you so then I have to tell you that plans are in hand (she underlines the word hand!) to ensure its continued expansion. Mr Oosterthing, she says, is working on other artificial aids which will make the medical world gasp. Well, thank heaven for that!

Basil

P.S. I have bought myself a little something in georgette!

St Cloud's

Dear Popsy,

If you ask me, Inigo doesn't deserve you. What an awful thing to have done. Soused herrings! I bet you could have screamed couldn't you? If Gemini ever did anything like that to me I would never speak to him again. Your best hat too. I know how you loved that hat, and it looked ever so sweet on you. He's just a filthy slut.

Basil

P.S. Gemini genuflected this evening and wrecked his corset!

St Cloud's

Dear Popsy,

Mother reports that trials of the leg have been completed (one dear thing walked 20 miles on it without so much as a whimper) and production will start as planned. I've told you, haven't I, that I am to attend the 'launching' ceremony?

Basil

P.S. Mother has received a letter from the chief of the Malubi tribe asking for two dozen Strollers in Vandyke brown. Isn't he a pet.

St Cloud's

Dear Popsy,

Have you seen the interview with Mother in this month's *Business Bulletin*? It's too utterly odd. She calls the Limbrub Stroller her 'baby' and says that Limbrub Ltd 'have a surprise in store for all those amputees who yearn to stand on tiptoe'! She also says that in some quarters she is being referred to as Our Lady of the Limbs!! Father Absolute says that if the Pope reads it he'll have kittens.

Basil

Dear Popsy,

I quite agree, Mother is behaving badly, but what can you expect from someone as selfish as she? If it were up to me, Popsy, you would have a seat on the board in an instant. In fact, if I had my way you would be chairman, with a big leather chair and a pretty pink blotter. You'd make a dreamy chairman.

Basil

P.S. I felt the sting of rawhide last night!

Dear Popsy,

Of course I will speak to Mother if you think it will do any good, though I doubt that it will. I keep telling you, Peachypie, she hates you. The only hope you have of getting on to the board is to give up Inigo, but could you do that? Could you desert your 'friend' and never see him again? Never, ever? Wouldn't it be the most awful wrench for you, Popsy, wouldn't it? Mind you, after that soused herrings business who could blame you if you were to leave him? Soused herrings! Was the smell too terrible?   Basil

Dear Popsy,

I'm sure you have made the right decision. Don't feel too beastly about it, Inigo is bound to find someone else before long (isn't he always 'meeting' people on Liverpool Street Station?) Should I write Mother the news or tell her when I see her?

Basil

P.S. Orders for the Stroller continue to flood in. One gets the impression from Mother's letters that she is quite rushed off her feet/foot with work.

P.P.S. Last night Nipper Thompson and Sir Geoffrey Grassington were partners in a Rialto two-step!

Dear Popsy,

'*Prepared*' to leave Inigo for a seat on the board? I'm sure if it were put like that Mother would regard it as blackmail and become obstinate. I think, perhaps, I should be a crafty kitten-cat and simply ask her what she would have you do before she found you acceptable. Mother is certain to suggest you give up Inigo and I would then write to you informing you of the condition. You, of course, would agree to it. This would make Mother think that she had forced you into doing something you had not wanted to do. A'n't I the cleverest minx you've ever set eyes on?

Basil

St Cloud's

Dear Popsy,

Thank you for saying I am clever. I hope when this is over you'll remember all that your boysie has done for you and make sure he doesn't go without the nice things he wants. What he would like more than anything in the world is a tea set painted with tiny dark violets and a pretty jade ring to wear.

Basil

St Cloud's

Dear Popsy,

Was it wise to tell Inigo that you intend leaving him? What if Mother decides she doesn't want you on the board at any price? Your black eye will have been for nothing. Oh, you poor dear, you. Does it hurt too much? Try placing a lump of raw porterhouse on it and afterwards a dab or two of Louisa Fryman's Cover-Up Girl – it's simply amazing how well it hides things. Gemini uses it all the time.

Basil

P.S. Be sure to keep your door locked at night.

St Cloud's

Dear Popsy,

Your letter made me want to rush straight to your bedside. Oh, Popsypoos, I should so like to be with you but with my Swiss trip coming up I simply haven't the time. Oh why didn't you keep your door locked as I advised? Will you be scarred for life? Gemini says scars are too romantic, particularly on the left side of the face. Thank heaven the surgeon managed to save your dear eye. Oh that beast Inigo, I could wring his neck, I really could.

Basil

P.S. The Brides send their love.

St Cloud's

Dear Popsy,

The briefest line before I leave. How are you? Are they treating you well? How is your dear face? Do you look ghastly? Thank goodness you've no parties to attend. No, I won't mention the incident to Mother, but how will you explain the scar? Perhaps you could say you were bitten by a wild dog. Oh, if only we still fought duels. I will write from Grenoble. Gemini says to keep your chins up!

Basil

Hotel Meisterhoff

Dear Popsy,

Grenoble is too gruesome for words – not a tuft of edelweiss to be seen. Mother and Mr Oosterthing took me along to the Matterhorn yesterday. It's quite pretty and ever so huge. The Stroller is launched tomorrow and I'm rather looking forward to it. Mother intends smashing a bottle of Dom Perignon against the first one off the assembly line. I haven't yet mentioned you-know-what as she hasn't been in too bright a mood. Do get better quickly.

Basil

P.S. Mother is wearing one of the rubber legs and positively cavorts!

Dear Popsy,

News to make your heart go tippy-tap! Mother is prepared to give you a third of her Limbrub shares provided you never again see Inigo Frick. You must now write to her agreeing the condition and she will have her legal people arrange things. There, you old saucepot, what did I tell you! A'n't I a blessing? You won't forget the tea set and ring (the ring must be jade) will you?

Basil

P.S. The launching ceremony went perfectly. Legs everywhere!

P.P.S. Limbrub Ltd has the most adorable lathe operator!

St Cloud's

Dear Popsy,

    The image of your poor face was with me from the time I left you to the time I arrived at St Cloud's. Oh, Popsy, I've never seen anyone look quite so ~~hideous~~ ghastly. Those bruises! I do hope they've all gone by the time you get this. Promise me you won't go back to that house for your clothes and things. Leave them there or let one of the servants collect them. If you go back Inigo will kill you.

Basil

St Cloud's

Dear Popsy,

    Are you quite sure you know what you are doing? How can you be certain Inigo will be out? What if he returns while you are there? Heavens, such a risk to take for a body belt. How you must love it.

Basil

P.S. Please make sure my tea set and ring are posted to me before you return to No.38.
P.P.S. I am aimless and broody tonight.

St Cloud's

Dear Popsy,

    The tea set is almost impossible (I asked for violets not anemones) but the ring! Oh, it's too scrumptious. It's quite made my life and I shall never take it from my finger. I look at it all the time and think, 'If only I had one for the other hand'! How I adore pretty things. How I'd love to be up to my young armpits in them. Thank you.

Basil

P.S. Mother writes that Mr Oosterthing has suggested she climbs the Matterhorn to attract publicity for the Stroller. She's thinking about it!
P.P.S. Last night I scourged myself with two sticks of rhubarb!

Dear Popsy,

How I'd love to see you in your patch. How dashing you must look. If ever I had a poor eye I'd wear a patch forever – blue gingham though, not black velvet. Just thinking of it makes me almost ache for glaucoma! How long will you stay in Grenoble? Do write me before you leave.

Basil

Dear Popsy,

I shouldn't worry too much about meeting Mother again; the Limbrub Stroller has quite made a new woman of her. However, do be careful not to mention the squishy noise she makes when she walks. Have you decided on a story to explain away the scar? Do think of something ever so romantic.

Basil

Dear Popsy,

Your letter with its darling little stamp has just this instant arrived, so I shall straightaway reply to it. Yes, I too wish I were there with you, though I don't know that I should care for all the walking you appear to be doing. Do the pines really remind you of me? Heavens, why? I simply loathe pines – they're so dishevelled. Perhaps that is why they remind you of me. Is it? I think I have gripe.

Basil

P.S. You're quite right in not dissuading Mother from climbing the Matterhorn. If she wants to climb a silly old mountain and fall off and leave all her Limbrub shares to us then let her do so.

87

St Cloud's

Dear Popsy,

Inigo Frick visited me today and made the beastliest of beastly scenes. He insisted on knowing where you were staying and when I told him you were at a false leg factory in Switzerland he nearly got hold of me. He called you the vilest names and said he would find you if it was the last thing he did. Under the circumstances perhaps you should delay your plans to return. He was ever so angry.

Basil

P.S. I think I'm in love with the Chocolate Coloured Coon.

St Cloud's

Dear Popsy,

At last a letter. But why have you returned when you know Inigo is after your blood? How brave. No, he hasn't been back here and I just pray that he stays away. I don't know what I should do if he were to return, I really don't. I have told the gatekeeper not to allow him in, but he (the gatekeeper) is so easily bribed. He'd do anything for a bottle of crème de menthe.

Basil

P.S. Grandmother Castleton's! Heavens, I think I'd rather face Inigo than stay there.

St Cloud's

Dear Popsy,

How utterly bored you seem. Are things too dreadfully dreary? Oh dear. Let us hope that Inigo will soon find himself a new friend so that my daddy can return to London and be happy again. Things here are ever so divine. This evening we (the Brides) have a party to attend at Sir Geoffrey Grassington's home. He's quite taken an interest in us – especially Nipper T!

Basil

St Cloud's

Dear Popsy,
      You cannot keep on the move like this, you'll wear
yourself out. If the smell of Grandmother Castleton is too
much to bear then you'll simply have to insist that she uses
something. Get her to try Louisa Fryman's Body Drench. It's
heavenly stuff and a large bottle will last for ages. Sir
Geoffrey's party was too ginsome. Everyone got awfully
squiffy and did the naughtiest things.

                                                                  Basil
P.S. Did you know that Sir Geoffrey collects suppositories?

St Cloud's

Dear Popsy,
      If you must return to London then I suppose you must,
but don't expect sympathy from me when Inigo finds you and
cuts your throat, because that is what will happen, I know it
will. Oh, if only Bletchworth were here to protect us. One
crack of his dear whip and Inigo would be off like a scared
rabbit.

                                                                  Basil
P.S. Limbrub shares are up threepence this morning.

St Cloud's

Dear Popsy,
      Father Absolute says that if you let him know where
Inigo 'hangs out' he (Father A) will arrange for a 'friendly
gentleman' of his acquaintance to meet up with him. Father A
says Inigo is sure to like the friendly gentleman as he is
6ft 3ins tall and 'built like a bull'! Father A also says that he
will require the sum of £50 to cover the cost of the arrangement. Oh, Popsy, isn't this the answer to our prayers? Send a
cheque and the information quickly.

                                                                  Basil

St Cloud's

Dear Popsy,

Father Absolute has passed the information to the Friendly Gentleman who has promised to be at Rose's Fine Bake every Thursday afternoon for the next three weeks. I must say, the Friendly Gentleman sounds an absolute dreampie. Heavens, built like a bull! I'm almost tempted to be at Rose's Fine Bake myself!

Basil

St Cloud's

Dear Popsy,

The Friendly Gentleman has made contact!!

Basil

St Cloud's

Dear Popsy,

The Friendly Gentleman moves in with Inigo next week so it is now quite safe for you to return to London. Ain't love grand!

Basil

P.S. Father Absolute says that should you ever again require his services he would be happy to offer them at similar rates. P.P.S. Mother writes that she has found herself a climbing instructor and is practising madly for the Matterhorn!

St Cloud's

Dear Popsy,

No, I do not think you should take Inigo's letter to the police. Inigo now has the Friendly Gentleman so it is unlikely that you will ever see him again. Heavens, what a fright it must have given you. 'Waiting in the dark with a knife'! Didn't you almost squeal with terror when you read it? I would have. I would have squealed my young head off.

Basil

Dear Popsy,

Has Mother told you . . . darling Mr Oosterthing has won the Design and Maintenance Golden Spanner Award! Isn't it just the most wonderfullest thing ever to have happened? Mother says Mr O is over the moon. When told the news he threw off his jacket and yodelled! The presentation is to be made next month at the Café Royal and Mother insists that I be there.

Basil

P.S. Will the spanner be made of real gold, do you suppose? What a pity it isn't a lathe or something, then we could *all* have a bit!

St Cloud's

Dear Popsy,

How should I know why Mother keeps you in the dark. Perhaps she hasn't quite forgiven you for the Inigo Frick business. As Father Absolute says, you can't kick a cow one minute and pump out whipped cream the next. Why don't you write to her and ask why you haven't been invited to the presentation. All I know is, *I* shall be there. My invitation card written in the prettiest gold letters arrived this morning. Ta ta!

Basil

St Cloud's

Dear Popsy,

What a joy it will be to see you again. Yes, of course you must meet me. I will let you know which train I shall be on. What will you wear? – for the presentation, I mean. Nothing too exotic. There can be only one pretty kitten-cat and it must be me! Gemini says he wouldn't be seen dead at a spanner presentation but he's just a jealous old slut, isn't he?

Basil

St Cloud's

Dear Popsy,

The Bruise, my horsey, is dead. Nipper Thompson heard the news from a local stable lad this evening. It seems the darling dear had to be shot after breaking a leg at yesterday's gallops. It really is quite odd because on Monday the leg of my chaise longue snapped off while I was romping on it with Gemini. It must have been an omen, though goodness knows in the heat of the moment the idea never occurred to me. My only thought, if I had one, was for my hair (Gemini can be so awfully careless when excited). I'm awfully upset about it – The Bruise's death I mean.

Basil

St Cloud's

Dear Popsy,

You too! Oh dear . . . Father Absolute did exactly the same, only the money he gambled with came from St Agnes the Divine's Restoration Fund. He's terribly furious, and says The Bruise has dropped him 'right in it'. Nipper Thompson says it serves you both right; ante-post betting, he says, is for the duffers.

Basil

P.S. Sir Geoffrey Grassington swears I'm 'the dead spit' of an Arab boy he once knew!

St Cloud's

Dear Popsy,

I almost forgot. You *must* write to my house tutor asking that I be allowed to attend the Golden Spanner presentation. If you don't, it is unlikely that I will be given permission. Don't delay. Mother writes that Mr Oosterthing has quite been inspired by the Golden Spanner and is now working on a de luxe model of the Limbrub Stroller. She says that if it turns out as good as Mr Oosterthing claims it will, she'll be able to *run* up the Matterhorn!

Basil

St Cloud's

Dear Popsy,
 The Head called me to his study today and told me that you had written him about the Spanner presentation. Thank you. He was awfully sweet and said the nicest things about the Limbrub Stroller. He also urged me to keep writing my poetry but suggested a change of subject!

Basil

P.S. The Head said that the governor of Bletchworth's asylum had written him saying that B was now showing a greater interest in his surroundings, particularly the asylum's leather workshop. That boy and his leather!

St Cloud's

Dear Popsy,
 No, I can't bear Debussy, but Mozart! Yes, yes, yes. Do you know his Clarinet Concerto in A? So vigorous! How wonderful if he'd written a rumba. Gemini's insane about him too, though his darling favourite is Mr Beethoven. Gemini says his Fifth is one of the duckiest things ever written.

Basil

P.S. Mother writes that the Limbrub Stroller is now the world's biggest selling false leg with 35% more sales than Ahab Supplies Ltd! Isn't it heaven.

St Cloud's

Dear Popsy,
 A musical evening at Sir Geoffrey Grassington's last night. What a scream! The 'artistes' were two gentlemen friends of Maurice Le Vere (Gemini said they must have been sixty if they were a day) who called themselves the Sisters Clegg. The songs they sang! The only one who wasn't blushing was Father Absolute. He said they quite brought back memories of his days as a novitiate!

Basil

St Cloud's
Dear Popsy,

Yes, one of the sisters did indeed have hairs on his/her nose (heaps and heaps of them) so it would appear that they are the very same Cleggs whom you once met. Heavens, you know simply everyone. By the bye, the evening following their 'performance' both were arrested for brawling over a tram driver they'd picked up! Guess who was chairman of the court they appeared in – Sir Geoffrey! He dismissed the case!

Basil

St Cloud's
Dear Popsy,

What a shock for you meeting Inigo like that. Didn't you almost die when he smiled? Are you sure it was a smile? Was his Friendly Gentleman really as huge as you say? Heavens, black! Father Absolute said nothing of his being black. Where does he find them! Just think, Popsy, that great big Zulu or whatever is now living in your dreamy little Chelsea house; pulling back your duchess satin sheets; touching the pretty knick knacks . . . Oh, how you must want to strangle him.

Basil

P.S. I was slippered by the gym master today for refusing to vault.

St Cloud's
Dear Popsy,

I shall be arriving 2.15 'but do not expect too much beauty' – I've had a beastly cold all week and it's quite wrecked my looks (not even Louisa Fryman has been able to help!). I'm sure to be famished so do let's visit a little restaurant for a bite to eat. I know you will say cook has prepared something but it's so much more fun eating out. It must, however, be the quickest of nibbles as I will need absolutely heaps of time to doll myself up for the ceremony. Should I wash my hair? I think not, it might flop. Oh dear, I do hope there'll be photographers, or do I? – my redness!

Basil

Dear Popsy,

What a pity that you had to dash away. Never mind, your boysie enjoyed himself ever so much; a scrumptious evening. How happy I was for dear Mr Oosterthing. I just wanted to weep when he was handed the spanner, and when those amputees sang 'We're gonna *walk* right up to those pearly gates' I felt the biggest shiver run right down my spine. Everything was quite perfect – well, almost. Why did Mother have to go on so about the beastly Matterhorn and her crampons? Heavens, it was all too embarrassing. Did you notice how, as we passed St Matilda's, she gazed at the steeple? Had there been a rope and grappling hook handy I'm sure she would have scampered up it!

Basil

Dear Popsy,

I would have thought you would have been glad that Mother is staying on in Switzerland. Heavens, you *must* be bored if you need *her* company! I'm sure if I were you I'd be having the most scrumptious time dressing up and everything. Oh, you simply don't know how lucky you are. Think of me and my beastly old school lessons. I can't have any fun at all.

Basil

P.S. This morning I received a photograph of Mr Oosterthing standing next to a pile of Limbrub Strollers (I thought at first they were dead bodies!) and holding his Spanner. He has written on the back 'To Basil, May one day you haff a golden spanner just like mine.' Isn't he a peach.

St Cloud's

Dear Popsy,

Yesterday we were set a poem to write so I wrote one on the Limbrub Stroller – Ode to An Artificial Leg. I'm awfully pleased with it and so, I think, is my English tutor. He has promised a book token to the boy whose work he considers best. Do keep your dear fingers crossed for me.

Basil

P.S. Gemini's poem was about Schiaparelli, but I doubt that it will win. The English tutor made the most ghastly face when he read the title.

St Cloud's

Dear Popsy,

News to make you pirouette! My poem has won the book token! The Head made the announcement at this morning's Thanksgiving Service. Oh Popsy, isn't it wonderful. I'm so happy I want to get ginned up to my roots! Imagine my surprise when the Head called out my name. You could have knocked me down with a feather boa! Gemini was awful. When my name was called all he said was 'Do you think my left eyebrow is higher than the right?' I could scream at him sometimes I really could.

Basil

St Cloud's

Dear Popsy,

There was no need to ask for a copy of the poem, I'd already planned to send you one – Mother too. I want everyone to see it, everyone! Oh Popsy, I simply must be a poet when I finish school, I must. I know I could be an awfully good one – not boring like old Masefield and Tennyson, but divine like darling Mr Whitman. Oh, how I wish the old dear were still with us so that I could send him something of mine to read. I'm sure he would say what the Brides are saying – 'Basil you are made for the Verse, *made* for it!'

Basil

Dear Popsy,

Mother writes that my poem is the nicest gift she has ever received and that as soon as it has been translated into French and German (!) copies of it will be pinned to the Limbrub notice board. Mr Oosterthing, she says, almost wept when he read it and to show his gratitude is now making a 2ft-high model of the Stroller which he will present to the school. I have told the Head this and he suggests that as St Cloud's is without a trophy for the 100 yards dash the model leg might well serve as such.

Basil

Dear Popsy,

All aquiver after meeting Inigo's Friendly Gentleman! Yes, he was here yesterday to see Father Absolute. Heavens, isn't he huge! Those shoulders! I should hate to be barged by him! Charlie, that's his name, took Gemini and me to dinner and afterwards to the Last Faerie for drinks. You should have seen Maurice Le Vere's eyes light up when we walked in – talk about lust at first sight!

Basil

P.S. Charlie seemed awfully fond of Gemini and told him he had 'de face ob an angel chile'! When he said that Gemini giggled like anything and said 'Not a Correggio, I hope'! Isn't he a caution.

Dear Popsy,

I have spoken to Father Absolute as you asked and he says that you are not to get your 'knickers in a twist'. Charlie hasn't split up with Inigo; on the contrary, they're as close, says Father A, as 'two fleas in a rat's armpit'! Charlie's only complaint is of Inigo's soufflés. He thinks them ghastly, but is teaching Inigo to make mango chutney and as soon as he has got the hang of it everything will be quite perfect.

Basil

P.S. Didn't *you* have trouble with Inigo's soufflés, or was it his omelettes?

P.P.S. Courtney Durham has just peeped over my shoulder and says the secret of making a good soufflé is not to use too much sugar!

St Cloud's

Dear Popsy,

Mr Oosterthing's model leg arrived this morning. Oo, it's such a ducky dear, you'd adore it. The Head does. He says any school would be proud to have it stand amongst its sports trophies. Father Absolute was a bit put out when I told him what it was to be used for. He recently had to sell a sepulchral urn to pay a gambling debt and wanted something to fill a niche in St Agnes the Divine's!

Basil

St Cloud's

Dear Popsy,

Guess whose photograph appears in this month's *Design and Maintenance*? Mine! I'm pictured on page 35 with Mother and Mr Oosterthing at the Golden Spanner presentation. Do dash out and get a copy. I'm practically in profile with my eyes half closed (how dark my lashes!) and looking too bored for words (I think Mother must have been talking about her crampons). Gemini says I look as though I had just seen my first Bernini!

Basil

P.S. I was lured into a navvy's cottage last night!

98

St Cloud's

Dear Popsy,

To Longmoor with the Brides last Sunday to visit dear Bletchworth. How well and happy he looked. He now works in the asylum's leathercraft section and was plaiting away like mad. Heaven knows what it was that he was making but I'm sure that it will be quite the prettiest thing ever. Longmoor's guv (he reeked of stout) is awfully pleased with B's progress and says that if he keeps it up he could be out in a little under 15 years.   Basil

St Cloud's

Dear Popsy,

If daddy rabbit is too utterly melancholic why doesn't he visit his baby bunny? Daddy rabbit could stay at the Last Faerie and meet baby bunny's friends – Nipper the gnat, Gemini the gerbil, Courtney the kitten, and Rory the rhino. If daddy rabbit does decide to come he must remember to bring heaps of money with him because baby bunny and his friends like lots and lots of gin to drink.

                                                                    Basil
P.S. Baby bunny was whipped last night by a man with one eye!

St Cloud's

Dear Popsy,

Saturday the 11th will be perfectly perfect. I have everything planned. I shall meet your train and we will straightaway go to my room where a surprise will be waiting. Afterwards to the Last Faerie (you have a room there with the dearest yellow curtains and a crucifix which has the words 'A gift from Brighton' carved upon it!) for another surprise, and later to Sir Geoffrey Grassington's for a party in your honour. You may, if you wish, spend the night at Sir Geoffrey's but don't be surprised if you find yourself having to share your bed with one of the guests!   Basil

Dear Popsy,

I do hope you are recovered. You looked so ill when you left Sir G's I feared you mightn't make it to the station. I had to spend the next two days in bed and was twice sick on my carpet. Honestly, I thought I was going to die. Gemini swears he saw Father Absolute pour something into the punch, and if it was the methylated spirit he carries with him it was no wonder we were in such a state. Didn't you think Nipper Thompson a scream? I don't know where he gets his nerve, I really don't. I nearly passed water when he tore off his frock and jumped into Sir Geoffrey's lap, didn't you?   Basil

Dear Popsy,

Your letter made me die, especially the part where you were sick against the wall. How kind of the woman to have helped you. As Father Absolute says, amongst the toerags there's always a silk stocking. I washed my hair this afternoon and combed it straight back, yes, straight back! Gemini said it left my profile too exposed so I quickly dried it and let it flop!
Basil
P.S. I haven't heard from Mother for three weeks. Do you think the Matterhorn might have claimed her?!

Dear Popsy,

Two letters from Mother today. She's in America with Mr Oosterthing for an international conference of artificial limb manufacturers. How beastly of her to go off without first letting us know. Thoughtless, that's what I call it. Anyway, she says Mr Oosterthing is quite the darling of New York and is having all kinds of honours heaped upon him. He is now a life member of The Foot in the Door Club and he and Mother are each to receive a diploma from the President of Miss Lovable Legs Inc. Gemini shuddered when I told him. He said Miss Lovable Legs stockings were the worst he'd ever worn!   Basil

St Cloud's

Dear Popsy,

    I agree, Mother should have told you of her trip, but just because she didn't doesn't mean that you have to be an old gloomypuss. Honestly, your letter was almost too depressing for words. If you want my opinion, you need cheering up and the best thing for that is one of cook's apricot pies. Why don't you get her to make you one (and one for me too!) and I'll bet you anything you like it will make you feel your old self again.

Basil

St Cloud's

Dear Popsy,

    When you send me food will you please make sure that it is properly packed. The apricot pie had to be thrown away because it was too squishy-squashy to eat. Perhaps you can get cook to make me another. Are you happier now? Your note was covered in lumps of apricot and quite impossible to read. I've just returned from the Last Faerie where I had a heavenly time with the Brides. Sir Geoffrey Grassington was there and said he would soon have an important announcement to make. Everyone's in a fever trying to guess what it can be.

Basil

St Cloud's

Dear Popsy,

    Please don't send me any more pies. I'm too utterly tired of opening parcels and having great bits of apricot splash on me. The last one you sent quite ruined a pair of gloves and I will now have to buy another pair. They cost an absolute fortune, you know. Did you read of the attempted escape at Longmoor? I'm sure Bletchworth must have been involved, because the newspapers said there was a 50-ft length of plaited leather tied to a window bar! Whatever will that boy get up to next!

Basil

101

St Cloud's

Dear Popsy,

If you send me one more apricot pie I shall simply lie
down and scream. The mess! My table lace is ruined as are two
pillow slips, an antimacassar (Courtney Durham took ages
embroidering it) and a darling veronica which Gemini gave
me. Really, Popsy, this is the third apricot pie in a week! Are
you deliberately being beastly to me?

Basil

P.S. Your note took two days to dry out and I was then only
able to read the part about Aunt Amethyst. Why on earth do
you want her staying with you?

St Cloud's

Dear Popsy,

Not an apricot pie for days. Thank heaven for that. I was
beginning to have nightmares about them! Mother writes that
she has enough orders from America to keep the Limbrub
assembly lines going day and night for a year. Isn't it too
wonderful. She also says that the final touches are being put to
the Stroller de Luxe and that production should commence
within the next six months. Mr Oosterthing is now working on
a hand which has a finger that beckons!!

Basil

P.S. How are you getting on with Aunt Amethyst? I do hope
she's a comfort.

St Cloud's

Dear Popsy,

Aunt Amethyst has written me saying she is concerned
for your health. She says that when she arrived cook told her
that you had had no sleep for a week and that she had been
rushed off her feet making apricot pies for you. Aunt Amethyst says she has never seen so many apricot pies – not even as a
girl. Are you ill, Popsy? I do hope not.

Basil

P.S. I don't think I ever want to wear anything but pink!

St Cloud's

Dear Popsy,

Your letter upset me for a whole day. I don't know what you mean when you say that everyone is against you. I'm not against you. Mother and Grandmother Castleton and Inigo Frick might be – in fact I'm quite certain they are – but I'm not. Heavens, Popsy, you must stop being so gloomy. As Father Absolute says, live for today and let the devil have tomorrow. Father Absolute thinks you are suffering from paranoia. Well, let's hope he's wrong. We don't want another one in Longmoor do we?! Are you taking the pills that the doctor has given you? You must, you know.   Basil

St Cloud's

Dear Popsy,

I am writing this during the maths period. Gemini is making a kiss curl and Courtney Durham is reading an article in *Soap and Home* entitled 'Do You Feel Guilty About Baby?'! Aren't they screams. Aunt Amethyst says that the pills are helping you to sleep. I'm so glad; there's nothing worse than not getting a good night's rest. I don't know about you, but if I don't get at least six hours my hair is quite impossible.

Basil

P.S. Gemini has just been given 200 lines!

St Cloud's

Dear Popsy,

Sir Geoffrey Grassington made his important announcement this evening. Oh heavens, it's so exciting! Popsy, Sir Geoffrey is to open a club, but wait . . . he wants the Brides to work in it! Honestly, we're in such a turmoil we can't think straight. The club (Sir G has already found premises) will cater for gentlemen only, and the Brides will work there at weekends and two nights a week. We don't yet know what our duties will be, but Maurice Le Vere, who is to be in charge, says we will be paid heaps of money. Sir G describes the club as 'a palace of joy'!   Basil

St Cloud's

Dear Popsy,

Just back from Sir Geoffrey's where more details of his club (we call it the Palace!) were given. Oh, heavens, he wants me for the Pain Room! Yes, there are to be rooms where his gentlemen 'clients' can be 'entertained'! Nipper Thompson is to be in Baby's Room and Father Absolute will hear 'confessions' in Holy Room. Sir G has told him that there will be occasions when he will be expected to dress as a nun! Gemini's duties haven't yet been decided upon but Sir G thinks he might be perfect for the Sabines' Suite! Rory O'Brien refuses to allow Courtney Durham to have anything to do with the project.

Basil

St Cloud's

Dear Popsy,

A peek at the Palace on Sunday. It's simply huge and stands in 20 acres of woodland about two miles from St Cloud's. Sir G is slightly worried that his clients will have trouble finding it so intends flying a flag from a turret. Gemini suggested that the flag have something rampant embroidered upon it which made Sir G cackle like anything. Because of the work going on (everything is being torn out in preparation for redecoration) there wasn't a great deal to see, but I was shown the room where I will be employed and you'll be thrilled to know that it has a ceiling in the rococo style. I waggled like anything when I saw it.

Basil

St Cloud's

Dear Popsy,

You can imagine how thrilled I was this morning to receive a huge parcel from America. I thought it might, perhaps, contain a dreamy Red Indian rug or a bunch of flamingo feathers, but out tumbled a beastly baseball bat and glove – gifts from Mother. I've never been so disappointed. How I enjoyed your last letter – not a bit of gloom in it. I suppose it must be the pills. Aunt Amethyst says they are anti-depressants and that you could become addicted to them. I do hope not.

Basil

P.S. Mother's ship docks at Le Havre on the 28th. She says the Americans were perfectly sweet, as were the Rocky Mountains!

St Cloud's

Dear Popsy,

Well, I have had my hair done and if you don't like it you can jolly well lump it, so there. I think it looks divine. Gemini has had his done too. Heavens, I've never seen so many waves. Gemini says they're enough to make even the Baltic jealous! Sorry to hear about your headaches. Are they awful? Try Louisa Fryman's Begone Dull Pain – it's too miraculous.

Basil

P.S. Mother cables from S.S. Aquitania that four of the passengers are wearing Limbrub Strollers – one a ten-year-old boy who came first in the three-legged race!

St Cloud's

Dear Popsy,

The whole of Sunday spent at the Palace advising Sir G on decor and such and talking to carpenters and plumbers and adorable little men with paint on their shoes. Bliss! Sir G allowed me a peek at the Pain Room where chains have been fixed to the walls and a huge hook with rope attached hung from the ceiling. Sir G says he has ordered a pretend furnace with ink branding irons and an oaken rack for those clients who may wish to stretch me! I can't wait! I have asked Sir G if I may have a brocaded scarlet divan to rest upon between sessions and he has agreed. Isn't he a peach.

Basil

Dear Popsy,

No, silly, I'm not really going to be stretched, just tightened a little. The cogs on the rack have been specially designed so that they cease to function after the first few turns of the handle. However, Sir G says that the 'rack operative' will not be aware of this and in order to help him attain maximum satisfaction I must make little moaning sounds and every now and then let out a scream. Honestly, Popsy, I was made for the rack, I know it.

Basil

St Cloud's

Dear Popsy,

I have sent you a stick of Louisa Fryman's Begone Dull Pain (you see, somebody does care for you despite what you say) which, if it doesn't clear your headaches, will at least make you smell nice! Ha, ha. What would we do without Louisa? Mother writes that she climbed 800ft last weekend and wore a hole in her Limbrub Stroller! Her climbing instructor has now advised her to wait until the de luxe model is available before attempting the Matterhorn.

Basil

St Cloud's

Dear Popsy,

Well, if Begone Dull Pain doesn't work I don't know what to suggest. Gemini says that whenever he feels headachey he goes out and buys himself something pretty. Courtney Durham is always getting headaches but that's only because of all the embroidery work he does. Heavens, the times I've heard Rory O'Brien tell him to put down his needle and rest his eyes, but he never listens, never. This evening I thought I saw a spot on my face. When I looked closer I found that the 'spot' was a dead baby fly that had somehow got stuck to the mirror. What a relief!

Basil

St Cloud's

Dear Popsy,

Heavenly fun with the Brides today. First with wild roses to Mrs Durham's elephant (a great lump of its trunk has been knocked off) and afterwards to the Palace where we drank tea with the workmen. How sweet they were. One of them wore leather braces which made me think of Gemini's gardener, Albert. Nipper Thompson was a great hit (everyone recognised him, despite his fur and make-up) and was asked all kinds of questions about racing. A young plasterer wanted to know if he received a special claiming allowance for wearing earrings (Nipper had on these huge pendants) and I thought oh, heavens, trouble, but Nipper, as cool as anything, turned to him and said, 'Up yours, dearie,' which had us all in fits and made the plastering youth blush like anything.

Basil

St Cloud's

Dear Popsy,

So you're being naughty and not taking your pills. Well, that's what Aunt Amethyst says. Oh Popsy, what are we to do with you? I have written to Mother telling her that you are unwell, though I doubt that she will much care. You know how she hates anyone who is sick. Do you remember the time I cut my knee and she told me not to be such a baby about it? I could have killed her, I really could have. Gemini and I took a stroll into town this evening and found Father Absolute simply reeling. He didn't even recognise us. I am reading Fanny Burney's *Evelina*. It's almost quite good, I think.

Basil

St Cloud's

Dear Popsy,

Mother comments on your sickness: What a man sows so let him reap. Heavens! She also says that if anyone should be ill she should be, what with the awful torments you have put her through over the years. Don't you just wish her crampons would fall off? Anyway, forget about old grizzleguts and let me tell you something to perk you up. I'm going to have a facial! Oo la la! Gemini knows this little parlour where for 15s and an hour under the lights they turn you into a proper little glamour puss. We go on Friday at 5 p.m.

Basil

108

Dear Popsy,

If you could see me now you would think I had just stepped from the pages of some dreamy beauty book. Yes, I have this minute returned from the face parlour and, honestly Popsy, look too scrumptious for words. I simply glow. I am not going to wash for a week and will sleep in an armchair so that nothing rubs off. Tonight I go to the Last Faerie where I will dance, and dance and dance.

Basil

P.S. How is your poor head?

Dear Popsy,

Since I last wrote to you I have:

A. Been given 200 lines for rolling my eyes during Thanksgiving Service
B. Bought a little something in printed crêpe!
C. Drawn a picture with a flower in it
D. Been lashed with a gaiter by a farmhand, and
E. Broken my comb.

The Palace looks prettier with each day. Work has now started on the Sabines' Suite and Gemini is there practically every evening advising on furnishings and decor. He is insisting on plum velvet drapes, damask silk wall covering and a marble fountain which squirts emerald water! Sir G made a face about the fountain and said clients might find it disconcerting but Gemini is adamant. He says he may need to freshen up between assaults!

Basil

St Cloud's

Dear Popsy,

Your letter cheered me up no end, though I was saddened to read of your new illness. Heavens, we are in the wars, aren't we? Yes, I am studying, and yes, I am attending church regularly (there's always something new to confess, isn't there?!) Did you see the letter in *The Times* about the Limbrub Stroller? Isn't it a thrill to know that we're appreciated! Mother says that production of the de luxe model will be delayed slightly because Mr Oosterthing wants to add hairs to the male leg! Mother says the hairs will come from the heads of novice nuns (10s. a sack) and will be an added comfort to our Catholic customers!

Basil

St Cloud's

Dear Popsy,

Just back from the Palace and a trial run on the rack. It fits like a glove!

Basil

St Cloud's

Dear Popsy,

I will do my best to visit you but I cannot say when. Honestly, Popsypoos, I haven't a moment . . . attendance every night at Sir G's parties (held mainly so that his Palace clients can look us over (Gemini says he's beginning to feel like a prize cow!)) and trips to the Palace to inspect furnishings, etc. No matter, my Popsy comes first. Thursday perhaps. There, I'll bet you anything you like you are feeling better already. Be sure to send me train and taxi money – and a little extra besides!

Basil

Dear Popsy,

A table at Fortnums! Yum, yum. Gemini's awfully put out that I'm going, but I've told him how unwell you are (Aunt Amethyst says she found you in the library talking to yourself!) and that he will have to do without me for a day. You should have seen the face he made! Basil

St Cloud's

Dear Popsy,

Cancel the table at Fortnum's, Gemini's booked me a perm! Basil

St Cloud's

Dear Popsy,

Aunt Amethyst has written me the most beastly letter. According to her I am a callous, ungrateful boy who deserves a good beating. She says that when I failed to turn up on Thursday I quite broke your heart and that you have been in floods ever since. Well, you can jolly well tell her from me that I couldn't turn up. As I explained, Gemini had booked me a perm. Anyway, how was I to know you would take it so badly? Heavens, it seems I can't do anything right. Basil

St Cloud's

Dear Popsy,

Aunt Amethyst says doctors are extremely concerned for your health and have advised you to enter a home for the insane (Aunt Amethyst calls it a home for the treatment of psychotic diseases but Gemini says it's just another name for asylum). Is it true? – what the doctors say, I mean. I can't believe that it is. I'm sure there's nothing wrong with you that a good night's rest wouldn't put right. DO GET SOME SLEEP!

Basil

P.S. I could eat jelly forever, couldn't you?

St Cloud's

Dear Popsy,

Your letter was all squiggly-scrawly and took me simply ages to read. Well, all I can say is what Gemini says and that is if you go into that beastly home you'll never come out again. Gemini also says that the patients have the most gruesome things done to them — like being thrown into barrels of iced water. Heavens, you don't want that to happen to you, do you? This evening to the Palace to view some curtaining though I don't know that I shall enjoy myself. Your letter has quite spoiled everything.

Basil

St Cloud's

Dear Popsy,

Aunt Amethyst writes that you went missing for two days and when you returned you were without a shoe and had no idea where you had been. Oh Popsy, why do you do it? Why? Haven't I enough worries of my own without having to worry about you too? Talking of my worries, the Head ticked me off about my hair today. He thought it 'too effete' and told me to do something with it. Well, I won't. If he thinks I'm going to comb it out after all the trouble I've gone to he's mistaken.

Basil

St Cloud's

Dear Popsy,

Your admittance to Peacehaven shook me to the very roots – and I don't mean the dyed ones either! Are you happier now? I wrote to the head doctor (is he a dream?) asking him not to throw any buckets of iced water over you and he wrote me the dearest letter back. It seems all you need is rest (didn't I tell you so?) and a little electrical treatment, whatever that is.

Your admittance made me think of Bletchworth in Longmoor.
How much luckier you are than he. At least you've a pretty
room with flowers and things in it. Aunt Amethyst says she
visits you whenever possible and I shall too, though not for
several weeks – I'm so awfully tied up (!) at the Palace. Aunt
Amethyst says she has written to Mother but has had no reply.

Basil

P.S. Try saying the following very quickly: Shut up the
shutters and sit in the shop.

St Cloud's

Dear Popsy,
    Please do not answer this if you're not up to it, and I don't
suppose that you are – not after that beastly electrical treatment. Aunt Amethyst has told me all about it and how brave
you have been. Did you get my flowers? I do hope the colours
were those that you most like. Mother writes that the Stroller
de luxe is coming along a treat and everyone is thrilled to bits
with it. Mr Oosterthing has asked her whether she wants hairs
on her model but she can't make up her mind!

Basil

P.S. I am wearing something a little Arabic tonight!

St Cloud's

Dear Popsy,
    I could not make any sense of your letter. Did you write it
before or after electrical treatment? What do you mean, it is all
lies about The Virgin? I only hope she can't read! With the
Brides to the Palace yesterday to see Gemini's fountain
installed. Heavens, the shape! You'd blush like anything if
you were to see it. It must be the biggest 'one' ever made!

Basil

113

St Cloud's

Dear Popsy,

I have written to Aunt Amethyst asking her to get you a bag of those crystallised violets that you're so fond of. Yum, yum. I myself have sent you a book which you may like. It is all about St Matilda of Westphalia and is quite a scream. The Head has been told of your condition (heaven knows by whom) and says he will pray for your speedy recovery. Isn't he a dear. The Palace is looking too gorgeous for words. Nipper Thompson has already taken up residence and says it's ever so comfy, though the noise of the fountain is driving him mad (oops, I shouldn't have said that word, should I?!).

Basil

St Cloud's

Dear Popsy,

Hello, how is my daddy today? Are you feeling better? No. Well you will be when you hear what I have to tell you. I shall be coming to see you on Saturday and I shall be bringing Gemini with me! There, isn't that good news? We will be arriving quite early – around 12 o'clock – but we won't be staying too long because Gemini has some shopping to do.

Basil

St Cloud's

Dear Popsy,

It was heaven seeing you again even though you were only half-conscious. Gemini said later that you were catatonic, whatever that is. I must say, you did look a bit down in the mouth. Just as we were leaving I heard someone cry out, 'Is that you Amanda?' and the next thing I knew this ghastly old man (he hadn't a tooth in his head) flung himself on me and tried to drag me to the ground. Honestly, I thought it was The End! Fortunately a huge nurse came along and pulled him off me. It was all too scary.

Basil

114

St Cloud's

Dear Popsy,
       I had rather hoped to have a letter from you by now but I dare say you are not up to writing. Oh well, we mustn't rush things, must we. Aunt Amethyst writes that she's awfully angry about the attack on me by that old madman and will take the matter up with the Superintendent. I fear he (the madman) may be in for additional electrical treatment! Did you enjoy the crystallised violets? I do hope you ate them all up because Aunt Amethyst had the most awful trouble finding them. She says next time you will have to make do with assorted toffees!

                                                            Basil

St Cloud's

Dear Popsy,
       How I wish your dear head was in proper order so that you could be here. Simply everything is divine . . . parties and outings and things . . . oh, it's heaven. To think that I once hated St Cloud's and begged you to take me away. Thank goodness you made me stay. How right you were, but then you always are. And now you are having a beastly time of it. Oh, it isn't fair – you who have never harmed a little fly. Are you sitting up yet? Is the electrical treatment helping? Gemini says that considering the number of times you have been plugged in it's a wonder you're not leaping about all over the place!

                                                            Basil

P.S. Heaven knows what I'm going to do for money what with your being unable to write and all.

115

St Cloud's

Dear Popsy,

If this news doesn't make you sit up, nothing will! I've won a house point! I know, I couldn't believe it myself! I got it for history. Heaven knows how, I can't tell one king from another! Gemini made a face when I told him. He hates it like anything if anyone does better than he. That's the only reason he insisted on having the fountain, because he knew I was to get a scarlet divan. Anyway, I'm sure you're pleased for your boysie. I do so want to make you proud of me. Oh, if only you could write or something.

Basil

St Cloud's

Dear Popsy,

Well, now there are two of us in the wars! I've a beastly sore throat and can hardly speak. All I do is croak, croak, croak – like a poor little froggy lost in the dark. Gemini says serves me right for going around half naked, cheeky thing! I was supposed to go to the Palace tonight to test the branding irons but I'm feeling so beastly that I think I'll stay in my room and suck a lozenge instead. Anyway, enough of me, how are you? Aunt Amethyst says she visited you again on Sunday (I don't know where she gets her energy from) and had a chat with the Superintendent who gave her tea and cake. She says the cake was stale.

Basil

St Cloud's

Dear Popsy,

Out today for the first time in a week (if you only knew how ill I've been. I think I've had pneumonia or something). Anyway, it was heaven to be in the open air again. Gemini and I took a little walk in a field and had tea with Nipper Thompson at the Palace. How splendid it looks. Gemini wanted to put me to the rack but I felt too weak so we put

Nipper to it instead. I think he quite enjoyed it! The workmen have started on Baby's Room (the Sabines' Suite is finished and looks perfectly divine) but are having difficulty with the wallpaper. Nipper Thompson wants ducks and boats but the workmen can get only balloons and trumpets. I hope you are feeling better and enjoyed this little card. It must be wonderful to have someone write to you when you are ill.

Basil

St Cloud's

Dear Popsy,

Still no letter. Oh dear, what am I going to do with you? My only correspondence these days is with Mother and Aunt Amethyst – and you know how dreary they are. Mother writes of legs and the Matterhorn (I wish she'd hurry up and climb the beastly thing) and Aunt Amethyst of her journeys to and from Peacehaven. If she complains once more about how busy she is I'll scream. Heavens, if she doesn't want to visit you why doesn't she say so. I'm off to the Palace tonight and haven't a thing to wear. Heigh ho, get out the rags.

Basil

St Cloud's

Dear Popsy,

Your being sick is quite hitting my pocket for six. I've no money for drinks or clothes or anything. What am I to do? I have asked Aunt Amethyst for a loan but she says she has nothing to spare, the liar. Heavens, the money she spends on that vile old face of hers. Popsy, you must help me. You must try to put some money in an envelope and have it posted to me. Could you do that, do you think? Could you get your wallet from that dear little cabinet by your bedside and send Boysie two £5 notes? I'm sure you could if you tried. DO HURRY!

Basil

P.S. I've just noticed that my bottle of Cutie Claws is practically empty!

118

St Cloud's

Dear Popsy,

A letter from your doctor this morning. He says that when my card was read to you you wept – the very first emotion you have shown since you entered Peacehaven. How wonderful. He also says that there is now hope of a full recovery (did you know that he was beginning to think of you as a 'goner'?!) and that I must continue to write to you even though I mayn't get a reply – well, not for a while anyway. The doctor is so pleased with your reaction to my card that he has sent me three £5 notes and a bottle of Cutie Claws. What a peach. He says he will add the £15 to your bill but that I may have the nail polish free of charge.

Basil

St Cloud's

Dear Popsy,

Our own Stroller de Luxe has been launched – yes, hairs and all! Isn't it too wonderful. Mother is ever so thrilled, as am I. Mother says the very first leg went to the President of Puerto Rico (an amputee for 15 years) who has returned it with a request that it be exchanged for a blond model! Mother is quite cross about it and says the last time she saw him he was as black as the ace of spades! Mother herself is now wearing the de luxe model (auburn) and says it's the best leg she's ever had, better even than her real one! She says she spent most of Monday standing on tiptoe!

Basil

St Cloud's

Dear Popsy,

Cooee! How is your poor brain? Aunt Amethyst tells me that the last time she saw you your eyes seemed not to stare so much. Is that a good sign? I do hope so. Gemini dared me to shriek during Thanksgiving Service! I did!

Basil

St Cloud's

Dear Popsy,

I am sending you by the same post a picture taken from this month's *Design and Maintenance* which shows the Stroller de Luxe in action. Do have one of your nurses pin it to the wall. The amputee is quite a peachypie, don't you think? I wouldn't mind having *him* stomp up my staircase! Mother says sales are simply furious and are quite exceeding all hopes. Isn't it grand.

Basil

P.S. Yesterday Gemini was in the quad putting on mascara when one of the tutors rushed up to him and gave him the most dreadful scolding. When he'd finished Gemini half closed his eyes and said, 'If that's the way you feel, you can have your ring back'! I nearly died.

St Cloud's

Dear Popsy,

Palace bulletin: Nipper Thompson now has the ducks and boats wallpaper he wanted; Father Absolute's Holy Room is nearing completion (you'll never believe what stands in one of the columbariums there!) and a dozen live rats have been let loose in the Pain Room. I shrieked like anything when I saw them, but they're quite sweet once they get to know you (there's one that looks exactly like Jane Austen!). Work on the lounge bar and cinema is due to start tomorrow so we could be 'open for business' in about six weeks. And how are you, ducks? Are you keeping well and doing as the dear doctor says? You must, you know.

Basil

P.S. I have had to ask your doctor to send me £10 and add it to your bill. You're going to owe heaps by the time you leave!

St Cloud's

Dear Popsy,

I've taken up bicycling. Oo, it's ever such fun. Yesterday
I cycled to town and back and didn't ache a bit. How fast I
went. How the trees flashed by. My young legs must have
looked a blur. Mother is in ecstasies over the Stroller de Luxe.
Orders, she says, are coming in thick and fast. She's even had
one from an American heiress whose pet ape was mutilated in
a revolving door! Aunt Amethyst says you screamed during
her last visit to you. Is that true?

Basil

St Cloud's

Dear Popsy,

How surprised you looked when I walked into your room (was it surprise? I do hope it wasn't anything else!) You twitched like anything, you know! In fact, for one awful moment I thought you were going to tumble right out of your bed. Thank goodness you didn't. I don't know what I should have done. You did seem a little happier than last time, though. Gracious, how you gobbled up your lunch – and the mess you made! I shouldn't care to be the nurse who has to clean your room! Before I left I spoke to the doctor who was ever so kind and said he was satisfied with your progress. I hope you don't mind but I charged another £10 to your bill.

Basil

St Cloud's

Dear Popsy,

I have, at Aunt Amethyst's request, written to Mother asking her to visit you. However, do not build up your hopes! Aunt Amethyst says she has written Mother dozens of times about your condition and the only reply she received was two lines requesting a book on the Matterhorn! I said in my letter that your mind has quite gone, but I cannot see that that will have much effect on Mother. Her beastly crampons come before everything these days, even your dear brain.

Basil

St Cloud's

Dear Popsy,

A divine day with the Brides and Sir Geoffrey at the Palace. The drink! Gemini and Nipper Thompson were both sick in the fountain and Father Absolute passed out in Baby's Room. Oh, if you could see it – the Palace, I mean. It's quite the loveliest thing ever. Sir Geoffrey says that when it is finished we can have a huge party and invite anyone we choose, provided of course that they are discreet. Oh Popsy, do try to get your brain in order so that you can attend. I could show you my rack and everything.

Basil

Dear Popsy,

Good news. Mother is *not* going to visit you. She says the Matterhorn must come first and nothing can be allowed to interrupt her climbing practice. She also says that you must stop behaving like a child (you see, just like the time when I cut my knee) and pull your mind together. She says that if her amputees knew of the fuss you are making they would quite be ashamed of you. We have a non dies on Friday so I'm off with the Brides to visit Bletchworth in *his* asylum! Life is one long scream!

Basil

Dear Popsy,

I'm so tired I can hardly keep my young eyes open. Honestly, since I last wrote you I haven't stopped – parties, paper chases and lunatic asylums . . . just one thing after another. It's a miracle I'm not dead. Still, it's all for a good cause, isn't it? And how is my daddy? Perkier, I hope. Our visit to Bletchworth was quite awful. He doesn't appear to have improved at all, though the governor is quite certain that he has. When we saw him he was sitting in a corner playing with a pile of dirt. It was too dreadful. Father Absolute said on the way back, 'If your old man could see that poor bleeder, he'd realise how lucky he is.' I had to agree with him, Popsy.

Basil

St Cloud's

Dear Popsy,

Why are people so awful? On Sunday at the Palace I told Gemini that I thought he was wearing a little too much mascara (honestly it was just like mud). Well, what do you think he did? He just looked me up and down and said, in that awful Don't Touch Me voice he sometimes uses, 'Tell me, Basil, does insanity run in your family?' Oh Popsy, you've no idea how beastly I felt. Fortunately Father Absolute reminded Gemini that half the world's most famous people were mad which made me feel ever so much better. Popsy, it just isn't fair. If you weren't in that place this never would have happened. That's why you have to get better, QUICKLY! You must be sane for my sake. Gemini has apologised and although I forgave him (well, what can you do when you're told that you look as fresh as a Canaletto!) I still feel beastly about it.

Basil

St Cloud's

Dear Popsy,

A gruesome letter from Mother this morning. She says that if you wish to keep your seat on the Limbrub board you must 'stop swinging the lead' at Peacehaven and get down to some hard work! She says Limbrub Ltd now has a 75% share of the false leg market but if greater sales are to be achieved she and Mr Oosterthing will need all the assistance they can get. She says 'a good war would help' but failing that 'we will have to roll up our sleeves and do the job ourselves'. She also says that if she is prepared to further the sales cause by mounting the Matterhorn then you too should be willing to lend a hand – even if it means helping out on the production line! Honestly, I don't know how she's got the nerve.

Basil

P.S. Tonight I wear something that rustles!

St Cloud's

Dear Popsy,

WHAT ARE THEY DOING TO YOU THERE? What are they doing to your BRAIN? Do try to write to me. Do try to THINK! Don't you want to get better? Don't you want to see your boysie in his palace? Oh Popsy, how you'd love it. Everything is so shiny and bright and I just ache to start work there. Sir Geoffrey says that it's cost him a fortune, what with the furnishings and chains and everything. Do you know, there's one chain in the Pain Room that must be 20ft long. Heaven knows what it will do to my young skin. I have told Sir Geoffrey that I will wear it only if he promises to line the collar with something soft. I think velveteen, or perhaps flannelette might do. What do you think? Gemini suggested sable but I'd simply bake in sable, I know I would.

Basil

St Cloud's

Dear Popsy,

You can scream all you like, but I won't care. I've borrowed £10 from your doctor and had him add it to your bill. Well, I simply have to have money. You can't expect me to stay alone in my room when everyone else is going out having fun; WELL, CAN YOU? Your doctor tells me you were taken for a walk in the gardens on Sunday. How lovely for you. Are the gardens pretty? They seemed not to be when I saw them. Tonight I inspect a massage machine which Sir Geoffrey is having installed in the Sabines' Suite. Gemini is objecting to it.

Basil

St Cloud's

Dear Popsy,

How nice to know that you have had visitors, although Grandmother Castleton is not someone I would care to see if I were ill. If only she would change that pinny. There must be enough mutton fat on it to grease a locomotive. It's too revolting. I'm sure that if one were to sit on her lap one would slide off! Aunt Amethyst said you seemed a little brighter but that your face was quite filthy. Heavens, I do hope you are being properly cleaned. I can't have my daddy looking like a vile old tramp. The Head says he has had encouraging reports of my work which he hopes will be of comfort to you. Isn't he a dream. I sometimes don't know how I stop myself from hugging him! Must hurtle, my new navvy awaits!

Basil

St Cloud's

Dear Popsy,

You'll probably hate me like anything, but I don't care if you do; I've added another £20 to your Peacehaven bill. Before you shriek let me say that the money will not be spent on myself. Most of it will go on shirts for my navvy (honestly, the poor dear hasn't a stitch to his old back) and the remainder on a trip to London. My navvy says that if he could once dine at the Café Royal he would 'die happy'. Well, who am I to deny him? I haven't a clue as to which colour shirts would best suit him. What hair he has is sort of beige and, as you know, beige isn't the easiest of colours to match. I'd love to see him in pinched avocado but quite honestly his complexion just isn't up to it. It's such a worry. Gemini says I should take him to an interior decorator!

Basil

Dear Popsy,

Heavens, what a time with my navvy at the Café R! Guess who was there – Aunt Amethyst! Honestly, her face when she saw us! She quite looked as though she'd swallowed a worm! I must say, my navvy's appearance what with his boots and avocado shirt (yes, I did put him in avocado after all) was a little outré. Aunt Amethyst and this gruesome old thing she was with didn't take their eyes off us. But that wasn't the worst of it. As we were about to leave Aunt A came across to our table and just stood there staring at me. It was too awful. In the end I did what Gemini sometimes does – I closed my eyes and ever so lightly touched my hair! When I looked again, she'd gone. What a cheek, though. I do hope you are feeling better.

Basil

Dear Popsy,

The sun popped out today so Gemini and I dashed to the seaside, and here we are. So far we've been for a stroll along the beach (Gemini found something vile floating in the moat of a sandcastle) and played miniature golf (I won!). We are now having tea in a bunshop and the waitress giggles every time she serves us. Gemini is becoming ever so cross and I wouldn't be a bit surprised if he says something to her. We haven't decided what we will do next but I have a feeling Gemini will suggest drinks at the Trawlerman's Retreat!

Basil

P.S. Gemini has just told the waitress that the tea cups smell of damp wilderbeest which has made her giggle like anything. I'm sure it's the rouge he's wearing.

St Cloud's

Dear Popsy,

I suppose you're cross with me for not having visited you. I haven't had a minute to spare, Popsy. The Palace opens in three weeks. And about time too! I shall be glad to get on the rack for a rest! You, of course, are getting heaps of rest, lucky thing. Are you speaking yet? I've told my navvy about you and he says his mother has the same trouble. She hasn't said a word for two years. My navvy says it doesn't much worry him because the only thing she said when she was speaking was 'Give us a tanner for a drop of gin, Albert'!

Basil

St Cloud's

Dear Popsy,

Aunt Amethyst tells me that when she visited you last week you drew a little picture for her. Well, what about me? Why haven't you drawn a little picture for me? Perhaps you feel that I haven't visited you often enough to deserve a picture. Well, all I can say is that Aunt Amethyst, unlike me, hasn't a beastly school to attend. I have to go on beastly paper chases and sit through hours of horrid maths lessons. I wonder if she would visit you as often as she does if she had to sit through hours of maths lessons. Anyway, who cares – draw as many pictures for her as you wish. I'll bet you one thing, though; I'll bet you that if you were to draw a picture for me I wouldn't describe it as 'hideously obscene'.

Basil

St Cloud's

Dear Popsy,

Your doctor, being the peach that he is, sent me one of your little drawings (heavens, does he read *everything* I write you?!). His thoughtfulness, however, almost landed me in the most frightful soup. I showed the drawing to Gemini during a history period and the History prof grabbed it. Well, the row! The prof said it was the most blasphemous thing he'd ever seen and took me straightaway to the Head. He thought *I* had drawn it! It took a telephone call to Peacehaven to calm things down. Heavens, Popsy, I've seen a few cheeky Cruficixions in my time but yours takes the cake! That centurion's spear!

Basil

P.S. Your doctor says the drawings are an indication that you are trying to communicate. Isn't that wonderful?

St Cloud's

Dear Popsy,

I cried today, I sat down and cried. I do not believe that I am a self-pitying person (despite what Gemini says) but today I felt so sorry for myself that I cried. I have no money; Mother doesn't care that I have no money, and my father – YES, YOU – is incapable of writing a cheque. Wouldn't you cry if you were me? It's all right for you, you have nurses and things to look after you. I haven't. I have to fend for my young self. Gemini refuses to help me (just wait until he wants my help) and Father Absolute is unable to because he's 'skint', or so he says. Well, you might as well know that I have today written to your doctor asking to send me £20 and add it to your bill, so there.
Basil

St Cloud's

Dear Popsy,

Chains, chains, chains! I want to spend my life in them! Yes, you've guessed, my first night's work at the Palace was a dream. Honestly, Popsy, I've never enjoyed anything quite so much – never. How my customers adored me – and the money! I'm simply rolling in it. One customer said I was the 'best' he'd ever had and tipped me £5. Mind you, the chains he had me wear! Houdini would have cringed! Sir Geoffrey is ever so pleased with us and is already talking of increasing our wages. He says exceptional performance deserves greater reward. Isn't he a dear.

Basil

129

P.S. Nipper Thompson's giant teddy bear has had to be restuffed. One of his customers threw a tantrum and took a penknife to it. The sawdust! Baby's Room looked like a butcher's shop!
P.P.S. Do get better soon.

St Cloud's

Dear Popsy,

Your note made me so happy that had I a drum I would have seized it and danced. Oh Popsy, you're back among the living! Thank heaven for the Volt! When will you leave that beastly place? When will you visit me? Let me know everything. I am having a lovely time at the Palace. Last night I was manacled for 2½ hours! My poor wrists! Gemini says I should wear something to protect them, but what I say is, if one enjoys a bit of pain why try to prevent it?! Ta ta!

Basil

St Cloud's

Dear Popsy,

You've simply no idea what heaven it is having you write to me. It's as though I had lost an old friend and found him again. What a pity you can't leave Peacehaven at once. Still, if the dear doctors say you must remain awhile then I suppose you must. As soon as I received your first note I wrote to Mother telling her that you were on the mend. She replied that the Stroller de Luxe was the amputees' No.1 choice and that the Matterhorn was calling her! Not a word about you. It's too awful of her. I'm off to the Palace tonight. Five customers, would you believe!

Basil

P.S. My navvy sends you his 'best'.
P.P.S. I popped into Gemini's room this evening and found him rougeing his toes!

130

Dear Popsy,

Your letter was so happy and bright, it quite made my day. How lucky you are. How wonderful if we could all be as happy as you. Heavens, just listen to me. Anyone would think that I was having a bad time of it. Well, as a matter of fact, I am. One of my customers has a passion for urchins and Sir Geoffrey has instructed me not to wash for a fortnight. I am now in my eighth day without soap, and absolutely reek. It's too awful. Simply no one will come near me, not even Gemini – least of all Gemini. He says he's always hated grime. Mercy, how I itch! Basil

Dear Popsy,

I write this in the bath surrounded by Louisa Fryman's costliest bubbles (Foam Sweet Foam, 3s.6d. a packet). Heavens, you've no idea what bliss it is to have my young limbs clean again. I have told Sir Geoffrey that in future if one of his customers wants an urchin boy he'll have to direct him to Whitechapel. I wouldn't have minded, but to go a fortnight without a wash and then have your customer complain that you're not filthy enough it just too much for a soul to bear. Yes, he actually complained! In the end I let him smear dirt into me. Honestly, what some people want for their money! Are you still making progress? Basil

Dear Popsy,

What a thrill to get your letter and to know that you are truly recovering. Mother writes that she is well (worse luck!) and that Mr Oosterthing has completed a working model of an artificial hand. Mother says it gives a thumbs up sign and has a finger which beckons!

Basil

P.S. You'll never guess who had me on the rack on Sunday – Lord Justice Cranbourne! When he'd finished tightening me he put a noose around my neck and made me confess to having done the most awful things to his nanny!

Dear Popsy,

What a pet you are being about the money. I hated having it added to your bill, but what else could I have done? It's so awful being penniless. Honestly, though, I never dreamed I had had *that* much! It must be these navvies of mine – they're so wildly extravagant! Aunt Amethyst says you will be staying with her when you leave Peacehaven. Is that true? Wouldn't it be wiser to take a holiday somewhere?

Basil

Dear Popsy,

I'm sure you're right; what you need is rest, and to stay at Aunt Amethyst's would be to exchange one madhouse for another. Gemini suggests an island, but I somehow can't see you on an island. I would have thought somewhere in Asia. One of my Palace customers has just returned from India and liked it ever so much. He said that what the natives won't do for a bar of soap is nobody's business! Must run – I'm off with Courtney Durham to see his stonemason. Mrs Durham's elephant is being ruined by vandals (there's hardly any trunk left) and the stonemason wants to discuss ways of protecting it. Courtney says he would like to surround it with barbed wire but doubts that the cemetery authority would permit it.

Basil

St Clouds

Dear Popsy,

Here am I slaving away on the rack and you're off to Monte Carlo. How I hate you! I suppose this time next week you'll be perched on some dreamy verandah with a young fish gutter or something by your side. Heaven! Do write to me every single day and think of me when you're having fun.

Basil

P.S. I cannot understand why you are popping into Lourdes. Surely you are recovered and no longer in need of a miracle – or are you just hoping for a peek at one?!

St Clouds

Dear Popsy,

Your letter arrived this morning and quite turned me emerald with envy. Is the sea really as blue as you say it is? How I should love to plash in it! Last night I was shackled for two hours and tonight I have my noose man back again, so you see, *some* of us have to work! What a pity about Lourdes. Let us hope that the outbreak will be contained and that you will be able to visit on your return journey. Mother is being beastly about my schoolwork and feels that I am not studying as hard as I should, soppy tart.

Basil

P.S. Have you seen anything there that you would like to buy for me? Some matching thing would be nice.

Dear Popsy,

I know I keep saying it, but it really is heaven having you write to me. The Brides and the Palace are a comfort, of course, but there are still times when one feels alone. What a dream it would be if I could be with you. I simply adore the sun and the sea, and oh, to visit a darling casino! We do have gambling at the Palace, but not roulette or anything like that – just strip poker. Sir Geoffrey was down to his underpants last night and looked quite revolting. Thank heavens he didn't win – I was the prize! Your description of St Charlotte's Madonna made me die. Would Wrinkle Vanish be of help to her, do you think?! Basil

Dear Popsy,

The picture postcard was sweet, and the stamp was sweet, but sweetest of all were the shirt and tie. The colour! The softness! I wore them for my navvy and he laughed and called me his little slut and then boxed my ears, the dear. How long will you be staying at Antibes? Forever I should think if it's as scrumptious as you say. One day, when I inherit the Limbrub fortune, I too will visit wonderful places. I too will drink from crystal goblets. Basil

Dear Popsy,

I really did do my bestest best to get away but the Head wouldn't hear of it. I'm sure Mother must have written to him because he complained about my work and said that I had already had too much free time. He also said my appearance was grotesque, cheeky thing. I do hope you had a comfortable journey and weren't sick or anything. I'll bet you're ever so brownish, aren't you? Gemini and I are off to an amateur theatrical this evening — *Hedda Gabler*. I'm sure I shall hate it – Henrik's such an old gloomypuss. Plays should be fun, I think, don't you? – like bathtime. Basil

St Clouds

Dear Popsy,

I'm sorry your journey was so gruesome and that you were ill. I think we'd better face up to it, Popsypoos, we're just a couple of old landlubbers you and I (remember what Lake Windermere did to me?). Gemini says he is never seasick which isn't surprising considering the number of trawlers he's been on! How awful about Lourdes. I suppose it will mean a mass burial in a lime pit or something. Ugh! It does make you think though, doesn't it? I mean, if one can't feel safe at Lourdes. . .

Basil

St Clouds

Dear Popsy,

You ask for my advice and I will give it. Do not visit Mother, she will put you to work on Limbrub's production line. Do not stay with Aunt Amethyst. She may have been kind to you in Peacehaven but she's as mad as a hatter and you've had quite enough madness for one year. Do not stay with Grandmother Castleton – she will complain about your Habit. No, Popsypoos, if I were you I would stay where you are. You have your friends at the club and should you become bored there's always the docks or something. You could, of course, visit me, but you must remember that I have my Palace commitments (the rack is my life now) and it is unlikely that I would be able to spend much time with you.

Basil

St Clouds

Dear Popsy,

You make me out a genius which, of course, I am not. However, it is nice to know that you have taken my advice and decided to stay in London. I'm sure you will find heaps of lovely things to do there. Now then, I've something screamy to tell you . . . I've a Palace customer who wears a Limbrub

Stroller (de luxe model). I think I passed out when I saw it (thank heaven I was chained up at the time otherwise I would have fallen and bumped my head). Anyway, when I'd recovered I told him about the company and how I had shares in it and everything, and the old dear was so thrilled that he slipped a £5 note into my halter!

Basil

St Clouds

Dear Popsy,

I'm so glad you liked the figurine. I know how much you adore Dresden so I simply had to get it for you. It cost me heaps, of course, but thanks to the Palace I can now afford these little luxuries. Yesterday I bought a truss for one of my favourite customers. He has this groin complaint but he's such a peach, and tips like mad. Tonight I have two of my regulars – one's an actor (quite well known!) and the other a former indigo planter. (You meet all sorts, don't you?) Well, what have you been up to? Are you getting out and about and enjoying yourself?

Basil

St Clouds

Dear Popsy,

I can understand your concern at your loss of appetite, but you must not worry about feeling languid. Heavens, there are days when I don't even want to look at myself! Do as cook says and try to get out more. They say walking is very good for one's constitution and you've always adored walking. How brave you were to have gone on those hikes of yours. Do you remember that darling little knapsack you always wore and how I would wave to you as you set off for Cumbria or something?

Basil

St Clouds

Dear Popsy,

So you would like to see Inigo again. Well, Father Absolute told me that Inigo's gentleman friend is a 'blade man' (that means he carries a knife) and if he catches you with Inigo he'll cut you up into little pieces. Do please stay away from him, Popsy.

I am so glad to hear that you are eating again, though I don't know what cook is doing by giving you Hungarian brawn. Yesterday at the Palace I had a huge plateful of smoked salmon. Honestly, I was so hungry. I think the rack gives me an appetite.

Basil

St Clouds

Dear Popsy,

Your letter made me both sad and happy. Sad, because you have chosen to ignore my advice and stay with Aunt Amethyst, and happy because you have decided not to seek out Inigo Frick. What a near miss. If Father Absolute hadn't told me about the gentleman friend you'd probably be mince-meat by now! When do you leave for Aunt Amethyst's? Heavens, I don't envy you one bit. Those ghastly parrots of hers, and those awful cold dumplings. Ugh!

Basil

P.S. One of Nipper Thompson's Palace customers gave him the most terrible spanking last night. The poor dear can hardly walk!

Dear Popsy,

Your letter made me die. Dumplings the very first day! Don't say I didn't warn you! Anyway, I'm glad to hear that you have settled in and are happier. Perhaps the countryside was what you needed. Do you recall the artificial hand Mr Oosterthing is designing? Well, Mother is so thrilled to bits with it that she plans to have it as the company's symbol. A drawing of it is to appear on all company notepaper and a huge working model (20ft high) is to be fixed to the factory roof with the beckoning finger directed at the Alps. I have told Mother that I am not happy with the idea and that a better symbol would be a leg. I mean to say, it was a leg which gave us our success, wasn't it?

Basil

Dear Popsy,

The woods sound heavenly as do the birds you peek at. I've never heard of a Pileated Woodpecker. Is it an English birdie, or has it popped over from somewhere for a little visit? All birds look the same to me, I'm afraid, although I do know a redbreast when I see one. There's one that perches on my window sill every morning. The mess! I could kill it. The only walking I do these days is in the Palace grounds and there are no birds there, well, not any pretty ones. Perhaps I should suggest to Sir Geoffrey that he has some brought in. Peacocks would be nice.

Basil

P.S. Courtney Durham was molested in a cake shop today.

Dear Popsy,

Well, you're a proper little ornithologist and no mistake! *The Times*! Fancy that! Honestly, though, I felt ever so proud when I saw your letter. I'll bet the experts are frightfully jealous. I thought it was too clever of you to have checked the reference books and things. A letter from Aunt Amethyst this morning. She says you still seem a little vague and that your muddy boots are quite becoming a nuisance – everywhere she looks she finds mud. On Sunday she found a lump under the piano and on Monday a lump on the sofa. She says things couldn't be worse if she were living in a trench!

Basil

St Clouds

Dear Popsy,

It's been ages since you last wrote. Are you all right? You haven't been gobbled up by a great crested grebe or anything, have you? I went to a party last night and it was ever such fun. There was a man there with a cat dyed purple. My navvy had a tiff with him because he was allowing the cat to drink from his glass. My navvy said it was 'proper disgusting' and so it was. Mother writes that the giant hand has now been fixed to the factory roof, but not without incident. When it was first put up something went wrong with the machinery and the beckoning finger was going at twice the speed required. Mother says it looked as though it was scratching rather than beckoning! However, all is now in order and everyone is thrilled to bits with it. Mother says that since its erection the Alps seem a little closer!

Basil

St Clouds

Dear Popsy,

You and your woods, how you go on about them. Don't you ever get tired of twigs and stuff? I'm glad you agree with me about the leg. I have since pointed out to Mother that in my opinion the symbol should incorporate *both* limbs – hand, with leg held aloft, perhaps. No, I haven't written any more poems – I simply don't get the time for them. I was going to write one on Genghis Khan but I went off him. Write soon.

Basil

St Clouds

Dear Popsy,

Isn't life odd; one day one is saying that one hasn't the time to write poems and the very next day one is sitting down writing one. Ode To My Navvy O, I've called it. I don't think it's one of my best but my navvy adores it and makes me recite it over and over to him, the luv. Gemini and I had a visitor yesterday – Albert, the gardener from The Clowts. He popped in to see us on his way to some grand flower show. Wasn't that sweet of him? Have you spotted any more rare birds? It must be wonderful to have binoculars.

Basil

St Clouds

Dear Popsy,

Your letter quite made me feel as though I were in the woods with you. I can just picture that dear little hedgehog among the hyacinth. I'll bet his mum didn't half tell him off when he got home! I'm sorry that Aunt Amethyst is being beastly about the mess, but I did warn you, didn't I? Can't you shake yourself before going in, or something? Sir Geoffrey gave us a little bonus on Sunday for our Palace work. Honestly, we haven't stopped, Nipper Thompson had eight nappy changes last night (eight!) and looks quite worn out, poor dear.

Basil

140

Dear Popsy,

It's not surprising that you have a chill considering the amount of time you spend in those damp old woods. Don't you think you should find yourself a different hobby? It can't be good for you, all that bird watching. I mean, apart from the health hazard it's so lonely, isn't it? I'm sure the birds are darlings, but they can't talk to you and make you laugh, can they? Why not find an interest which would bring you into contact with other people – amateur theatricals or something. Wouldn't you like that – to be tarted up on stage with the audience cheering and everything? I would. Mother writes that the Basel Museum of Modern Science have heard she is to climb the Matterhorn and are asking if they might have her leg (the false one, of course) for exhibition once the conquest has been made. Mother says she's thinking about it.

Basil

Dear Popsy,

Please don't get upset. If bird watching makes you happy then by all means continue with it. Heavens, what a fuss over a few beastly birds! I am glad to know that your chill is on the wane. Do remember when you next go bird watching to wear something that will keep out the nasty old damps. I had everyone in fits yesterday. The History prof asked if anyone knew how Henry VIII died. Well, I quickly ut up my hand and said that he was shot in the eye with an arrow. Honestly, I'm hopeless at history, I really am.

Basil

St Clouds

Dear Popsy,

Had you told me of your appointment sooner I should have asked the Head for the day off and we could have met in London for lunch or something. However, I do hope that all went well and that the dear doctors are satisfied with your progress. (You didn't tell them about the midnight bird watching, did you? I do hope not.) By the bye, you might be interested to know that my navvy keeps birds – pigeons. Isn't that sweet? He has heaps of them and I'm forever brushing bits of feathers from his coat collar which makes him ever so cross. Perhaps you and he should meet and exchange birdy stories.   Basil

St Clouds

Dear Popsy,

I'm so glad you enjoyed your visit to Peacehaven. It's odd the kind of places one sometimes misses. I suppose you felt safe there or something. I'm sure that when I leave St Cloud's I shall miss it quite desperately. How strange of the doctors not to have commented on your progress; still, you know what doctors are – it's always a penny for their thoughts, isn't it? I hate doctors, they think they know everything. Mother writes that the Stroller de Luxe sales are spiralling and that Ahab Supplies have let it be known that they are interested in being bought out. Isn't that wonderful?   Basil

St Clouds

Dear Popsy,

Is it wise to be going to the fens alone? Wouldn't it be sensible if you were to take Aunt Amethyst with you? I know she's gruesome but at least you'd have someone to talk to when you're not watching whatever it is you're going to watch. You must consider your health, Popsy. I'm sure if your doctors knew what you were planning they'd scream like anything. Gemini and I went shopping yesterday and spent simply heaps. Honestly, the price of things! You'd swoon if you knew how much I paid for a hat.   Basil

St Clouds

Dear Popsy,
Thank you for the pretty feather. The colour is exactly that of Louisa Fryman's newest hair rinse – Copper Topper – which is all the rage here. Simply everyone is copper! I am using it (the feather) as a book mark so will think of you and the fens (and Louisa!) every time I turn a page. Weren't you scared when you became lost in the dark? I should have been. Aunt Amethyst wrote while you were away and said she expected you'd bring half the fens back with you! I do hope you did! I look the most awful sight today.

Basil

St Clouds

Dear Popsy,
I sneezed twice this evening but I don't think I have a cold. Aunt Amethyst tells me that you have been teaching her parrots to make cuckoo noises. She's awfully upset about it and asks me to try to persuade you to return to London. I think it might be a good idea, Popsy – to return to London, I mean. You know what Aunt Amethyst is like – she'd have you committed before you could say Jaquetta Robinson! The Brides screamed when I told them about the parrots. Father Absolute said *you* sounded a bit cuckoo yourself! Will you return to London? Say yes to Boysie. It would get you away from those beastly old woods and perhaps prevent a relapse. It would also mean that I could pop down to see you from time to time. Wouldn't you like that? Yes, of course you would.

Basil

P.S. A man was horrid to me last night so my navvy hit him with a piece of lead piping!

St Clouds

Dear Popsy,

Your story differs from the one Aunt Amethyst tells. Aunt Amethyst says she *ordered* you to leave. Is someone fibbing to Boysie? No matter, you are back in London and that is what counts. Yes, I'm sure you do miss the woods and birds, but you will soon forget them. How sweet of cook to have made your favourite pie. She is a dear old thing sometimes. I was given a hundred lines today for looking at my hands. I don't know what the world is coming to!

Basil

St Clouds

Dear Popsy,

How wonderful that you are getting out and about. However, you must not tire yourself. Is it wise to visit the zoological gardens quite as often as you do? I'm sure the baboons are dears but one can have too much of them, don't you think? You'll never guess who was at the Palace last night – Inky Pryce! There was I tarting myself up in the Pain Room when in he walked. Well, I don't mind telling you, my first impulse was to go straight up to him and give him a piece of my mind (about The Bruise and everything) but I thought no, Basil, let's have some fun with the old beast. So I waited until he was saddled and blinkered (he'd brought this caseful of riding stuff) then I mounted and thrashed him to bits. Honestly, by the time I'd finished he looked quite Regency wallpaperish – all pink and striped!

Basil

144

Dear Popsy,

I shall be in London with my navvy early Saturday (around 11 a.m.) so please meet us. My navvy wants to visit Trafalgar Square (him and his pigeons!) and afterwards Lilley & Skinner for a new pair of boots. Perhaps we could have lunch. I will not be able to stay late because I'm on at the Palace at 7.30 so no tempting me with theatres and things! Have you been enjoying yourself? It's heaven to know that the doctors are pleased with your progress. How right you were to have left Aunt Amethyst's. Those filthy woods would have been the death of you. Mother writes that she is quite ready for the Matterhorn but climbing conditions are unfavourable and likely to remain so for some time.

Basil

P.S. My navvy says he's proper looking forward to meeting you!

St Clouds

Dear Popsy,

Yes, yes, I know about Bletchworth. Isn't it too exciting. We've had the police here every day this week and the whole school is quite in a turmoil. Did you know that B left a note for Longmoor's guv saying he would like to cut out his (the guv's) liver?! What a scream! My navvy says that Bletchworth must be a 'proper fly one' because Longmoor is ever so difficult to escape from. The police have told us that if Bletchworth contacts any of us we are to let them know immediately. Some hope! If Bletchworth contacts me I will run to him, RUN! Thank you for a heavenly Saturday.

Basil

St Clouds

Dear Popsy,

I agree with you about the newspapers – they're being too beastly. Did you see *The Times* – 'Search widens for maniac schoolboy'. Maniac, I ask you! B's as sane as you and I. The police continue to watch the school and have warned people living nearby to bolt their doors at night. Honestly, anyone would think a wild puma or something was on the loose. Sir Geoffrey is awfully worried that with so many policemen about Palace trade might suffer but so far only the noose man has stayed away, which I don't mind a bit – he's been getting terribly reckless with the rope recently (you should have seen my neck last week – raw as anything it was). Do keep your fingers crossed for B.   Basil

St Clouds

Dear Popsy,

Do not panic, and for heavens sake DO NOT CALL THE POLICE. If you do I will never speak to you again. I shall be with you as soon as possible. Give B the biggest hug for me.

                                                        Basil
P.S. I suggest the attic as a hiding place, not the summer house, the boy will catch his death there.

St Clouds

Dear Popsy,

The Head gave me the most awful ticking off when I got back, but faugh to him; I saw B and that is all that matters. Have you given any more thought to getting him out of the country? I still believe my plan to be the safest. Whatever you decide, do act quickly. There is now, so my navvy tells me, a reward of £200 for B's capture.

                                                        Basil
P.S. Tell B I have had the weals surrounded with an iodine heart – he will understand.

Dear Popsy,

Do you hate me? I wouldn't blame you. The police were horrid to me and threatened all sorts of beastly things if I refused to tell them what they wanted to know. If only I were stronger. I have told my navvy I never want to see him again and that I hope the reward money will bring him nothing but misery. I will try to visit you as soon as the prison people allow, but only if you want to see me. Do you? I'd die if you didn't. Whatever happens I will be at your court hearing and will even be a witness for you if you think it will do any good. I haven't stopped crying for two whole days. Heaven knows what my Palace customers will think when they see me with my face all puffed up and everything. I am too upset to write more.

Basil

P.S. Mother writes that we now own Ahab Supplies Ltd. Isn't that grand.

P.P.S. *The Times* spelt your name with two t's!

Dear Popsy,

You are, without doubt, the kindest, most forgiving daddyplum in the whole world. Your poor little letter made me weep with shame and I promise you that from now on I will study like anything. I do hope your counsel is right, but try not to be too disappointed if the sentence is a little heavier than the six months he expects. One of my legal clients at the Palace thinks it more likely that you will be j----- for 12 months. However, do not think about it. Keep your chin up and write as often as you can.

Basil

Dear Popsy,

I am sending you some chewing tobacco which Father Absolute says is ideal for bribing the 'screws' (prison warders). Apparently they all love it! My navvy called on me last night but I had the gatekeeper turn him away. I simply hate him.

Basil

P.S. Aunt Amethyst has written saying she wants nothing more to do with you. I have replied that you are better off without her.

P.P.S. Everyone here thinks you a hero!

St Clouds

Dear Popsy,

I read in *The Times* of your court appearance and felt ever so guilty at not being there. Was it too beastly? I'll bet you felt an awful lemon, didn't you? My man at the Palace says there will next be a committal hearing and you will then be ordered to stand trial, but I expect your counsel has already told you this. I have heaps of messages. Your dear doctor at Peacehaven asks me to wish you good luck and I've even had a note from Mr Oosterthing who wishes you 'bon voyage'!! (Nothing from Mother.) The Brides, of course, all send you their best, as does Sir Geoffrey. Aren't they treasures, every last one of them?

Basil

St Clouds

Dear Popsy,

How are you coping in B-i-t-n? You haven't told me about your cell or anything. Oh, you poor dear, I'll bet it's awfully bleak, isn't it? Father Absolute says you have to use a potty (ugh!). My navvy keeps pestering me, but I cannot bring myself to speak to him, I know I shouldn't, but I do feel sorry for him at times. He looks so lost, poor luv.

Basil

St Clouds

Dear Popsy,

After I left you I went to a tiny nearby park and almost howled. Oh Popsy, it was too awful seeing you in that horrid place. Let us pray that you are soon released and that you will be able to forget all the beastly things that have happened to you. I have told the Head of your court appearance next week and he has said that if I wish I may take a few days off. However, I have decided not to accept the offer. Well, I can't let the poor Palace luvs down, can I? Don't be too gloomy.

Basil

St Clouds

Dear Popsy,

Have you had all the bits and pieces that you asked for? I left the list with Edwards and he said he would attend to it immediately. I mentioned the smell-killing thing to him but he seemed not to understand. However, Courtney Durham says the product was written about in a recent edition of *Soap and Home* which he is trying to find. In the meantime I have sent you a lovable little veronica doused with Louisa Fryman's Midnight Romps. Perhaps you can hang it in your cell. Look for me in court.

Basil

St Clouds

Dear Popsy,

I tried to speak to you after the hearing but the beastly court people wouldn't allow me near you. Do not feel too downhearted at the result. I'm sure your trial will be a success and that you will be found not guilty. My Palace judge thinks you might have to wait quite a long time for the trial – anything up to a month – so do try to keep your dear mind occupied. Have you books to read? Father Absolute says some prison libraries are frightfully well stocked (he seems to know an awful lot about prisons!) but urges you to avoid *The Water Babies*. He says the illustrations will quite turn a prisoner's mind!

Basil

P.S. Mother writes that she hopes you get 10 years!

St Clouds

Dear Popsy,

I do hope you have settled in a little. I know it must be horrid for you (the other prisoners sound too ghastly, especially the one who called you a name) but keep saying over and over, 'I'll soon be free, I'll soon be FREE!' You will, you know – be free, I mean. My navvy (yes, I'm back with him! He came calling on me with the sweetest of gifts (I hope it wasn't bought with the reward money!) and I simply couldn't turn him away) says you're a proper gent and courts don't convict gents. It's only the likes of him, he says, as gets sent down. He's right, Popsy, you are a proper gent, and you won't be convicted, I just know you won't.

Basil

St Clouds

Dear Popsy,

I'm sorry you feel as you do about my navvy. Yes, he did betray you, but haven't you always taught me to forgive and forget? Anyway, he's ever so sorry and says that if he could change places with you he would. I think that's rather sweet. The luv would like to visit you but I have told him that he should wait until you are more settled. Do let me know if there is anything that you need – a book or a cake?

Basil

Dear Popsy,

The Old Bailey, how lovely! Aren't you simply thrilled to bits? I am, I think it's too Doctor Crippenish, I really do. What a pity you won't be in No.1 Court. I'm sorry you haven't yet found anyone to chum up with, but I'm sure you will. I suppose one's first taste of prison is rather like starting school – one imagines that one will never find a chum, but one always does. I'm so glad your counsel is optimistic about the trial but then counsels usually are, aren't they? I mean, he's hardly likely to tell you there's no hope, is he? Do keep your pecker up and do let me know as soon as your trial is fixed. One must make arrangements!

Basil

P.S. I discovered today what my navvy bought with part of the reward money – a new pigeon loft! I sometimes think he thinks more of his pigeons than he does of me!

P.P.S. I'll bet Bletchworth's ever so jealous that you're at the Old Bailey.

St Clouds

Dear Popsy,

Yes, yes, of course I will be at your trial. Try keeping me away! What a relief for you now that you know when it is to be. Has your counsel told you what you must do in court – where to put your hands, and that sort of thing? Heavens, I do hope he's as clever as you say. Father Absolute has doubts. Father Absolute says there's only *one* 'mouthpiece' for you and that's Sir Marcus Pilkington. I suppose it's too late to send for him?

Basil

St Clouds

Dear Popsy,

Look for me in the gallery. I'll be waving like mad! Good luck!

Basil

St Clouds

Dear Popsy,

   Courage. Iron bars do not a prison make. Think only of
the day when you will be released. Father Absolute says that if
you keep your 'nose clean' you could be out in little under a
year. Do try – to keep your nose clean, I mean. No ragging
anyone's cell or anything. Father Absolute also says that you
must get to know the 'snout baron' (the man with the tobacco)
who will protect you from attacks and provide you with little
comforts. Are you to stay in Brixton? Father A thinks you
might be moved to Wandsworth. He says it's really awful
there. Guess who Gemini and I saw leaving the courtroom?
Inigo Frick and his gentleman friend. Inigo was giggling like
anything, and I overheard him say 'Serve the bitch right'. For
two pins I would have slapped his beastly face.

Baoil

P.S. Did you hear a scream as you were sentenced? That was
me. Gemini pretended to put a spider on my neck!

St Clouds

Dear Popsy,

   You poor luv. How ghastly and dreary and everything for
you. I think I'd die if I had only ping pong to look forward to.
We have ping pong here and I hate it. Try not to let slopping
out upset you too much. Father Absolute says you will soon
get used to it. He says the secret is to think of it as giblet
broth, but you hate giblet broth, don't you. A letter arrived
from Mother this morning. She fears that the sensation of your
imprisonment will have an adverse effect on Limbrub sales
and insists that you give up your place on the board. She says
the sooner she is up the Matterhorn and away from the scandal
the better she will feel. I just hope she falls off and breaks her
beastly old neck, don't you?

Basil

P.S. What is it that you do in the laundry?

152

St Clouds

Dear Popsy,

How I gobbled up your letter. Your chum Sid sounds divine. How thrilling it must be to have a bank robber sleeping alongside one. I'll bet it makes you feel ever so safe (ha, ha) doesn't it? Do try to eat up your food. It may be vile but we can't have you looking like Nancy Cunard, can we? I too have a calendar (I'm sure yours is prettier) and will cross off the days with you. I have worked it out that you still have 433 days to serve. Is that what you make it? Heavens, I'll be quite an old thing by the time you get out! Your laundry work sounds too gruesome. How damp you must be with all that steam. Does it make your hair go limp and everything?

Basil

P.S. Do give Sid my fondest wishes. Twelve years! The poor dear.

P.P.S. Father Absolute asks if Sid's second name is Cartwright. He says if it is tell him that he (Father A) is still waiting for his 'cut' from the Hampstead job!

St Clouds

Dear Popsy,

Did Sid really laugh at my little joke? How wonderful. I have told Father Absolute that he (Sid) is not a Cartwright but Father A is not convinced. He asks if Sid has a missing finger on his left hand. Has he? Talking of hands and things, Mother wants to know if you have any amputees there who would be interested in receiving literature on the Stroller de Luxe. I think it's too awful of her to ask, don't you? I am so glad you have found a 'screw' who is helpful. It makes such a difference to have someone in charge who is not being beastly to one the whole time. Courtney Durham and Rory O'Brien have bought a cottage by the seaside so as soon as I can arrange time off from the Palace I shall pop down to see it. Courtney says it's a bit tumbledy-wumbledy at the moment but is having workmen in to paint it and make it pretty.

Basil

P.S. Isn't it possible to transfer from the laundry to a less horrid job? I'm sure you have only to ask nicely.

St Clouds

Dear Popsy,

Your poor hands. I had planned to send you a pot of Louisa Fryman's Pretty Paws to soothe away the pain, but Father Absolute tells me that prisoners are not allowed to receive gifts. How mean! He suggests that before going to bed you bind your hands in rags smeared with axle grease. He says a week of this treatment and the soreness will quite be gone. I'd adore to see the matchstick house you are building. Does it have little windows and things? It's scrumptious to know that you are getting on so well with Sid. Would he like me do you think? On Saturday I'm off with my navvy to Courtney Durham's seaside cottage. My navvy says that as soon as we get there he will buy me a bowl of whelks! He says they are proper tasty.

Basil

Dear Popsy,

I have passed on your thanks to Father Absolute who says he is only too happy to be of help. What a treasure he is. One of his Palace customers is so impressed with his (Father A's) service that he is now thinking of becoming a convert. Father A laughed when he told us and said the customer was getting his pervs mixed up with his cons, but I think it's wonderful. Anyway, your hands are better, which is good news. Courtney Durham's cottage is too dreamy for words – thatch everywhere and almond trees in the garden. I'm sure he and Rory will be ever so happy there. My navvy says he would like one (a cottage) for us! I'm so glad you've joined in the ping-pong games. One mustn't be an outsider, must one? Have fun.

Basil

P.S. Gemini and I get out the raspberry jam tonight. It's been such a long time.

Dear Popsy,

What adventures you do have. Honestly, your letters make the stories in *Soap and Home* seem quite dreary-weary. How I wish you could write to me more often. How I wish I could be there with you. Yes, in prison! Did you really meet an acid thrower? How thrilling. Didn't you almost want to turn your face away, just in case?! I think it's beastly that no one speaks to the child molesters. Heavens, if it wasn't for them we'd have to close down the Palace! Basil

Dear Popsy,

I must say, Sid's fits of temper do seem rather disturbing. Fancy him punching that old lag like that. Father Absolute fears that Sid may be drinking boot polish (ugh!) which would account for his aggressiveness. Do try to get him to break the habit, Popsy – for your own sake. Gemini and I visit Bletchworth next week. Would you like me to give him your love?

Basil

155

Dear Popsy,

How disappointed I was not to have a letter from you this week. I suppose you used up your 'ration' on someone else, naughty thing. On Sunday Gemini and I visited Bletchworth and were quite surprised to see how fat he has grown. Talk about roly poly! The governor said he thought it was due to a new-found contentment, and I must say, the boy did seem the happiest of creatures. How he laughed when he saw us. I thought he would never stop. Over tea I told him what had happened to you and he laughed so much I feared he might injure himself. The strange thing was that during the whole of the time we were with him he never spoke a word, even when he gave me a dear little cardboard box he had made. Gemini said later that it was the worst cardboard box he had ever seen, but I will treasure it.

Basil

Dear Popsy,

If it hadn't come from your own pencil I never would have believed it. You, brawling! Whatever next! Well, as far as I am concerned Sid jolly well deserved all he got. He had no right to break your things. Did you really 'put the boot in'? (Honestly Popsy, some of the jargon you use! Thank heaven I have Father Absolute to translate for me.) I think it too horrid of them to have stopped your privileges for a week and if I were you I would complain to the authorities about it. Father Absolute says the incident will now be entered on your record card and could go against you when you are considered for early release. Oh dear, if it's not one thing it's another. I told my Palace judge what happened and he thinks that you are becoming brutalized. So soon!

Basil

St Clouds

Dear Popsy,

You don't have to tell *me* how easy it is to pick up other people's habits (heavens, before I came here I never would have dreamed of having my eggs boiled in eau de cologne) but there are nice habits and there are nasty ones. Do try to avoid some of the nasty ones, Popsy. How thrilled you must have been meeting the Snout Baron. He sounds a peach (calling you a toff and all) as does his boy prisoner. Father Absolute thinks that he (the Snout Baron) has taken a liking to you. So you *have* found a chum. Didn't I tell you so. Didn't I?

Basil

St Cloud's

Dear Popsy,

No, you do not shock me. I quite understand your happiness. Before your imprisonment you had no friends and were always being picked on by Mother and her beastly family. Now you have heaps of friends and are awfully popular (I think it wonderful that everyone calls you The Toff and that you are winning all your fights). You have found a real home. But remember, Popsy, you won't be in prison forever. One day you will be released (I have worked it out that you have 463 days to serve) and will again have to face the outside world. It is something you must prepare yourself for. Promise me you will. I should hate it if you were to leave prison and go straight back to Peacehaven.

Basil

P.S. Mother writes that the Stroller de Luxe has won the Parchment d'Honneur at the Paris Trade Festival. The Crown of Laurels went to a machine that peels potatoes. Mother says it's a scandal.

157

St Cloud's

Dear Popsy,

Thank you for saying kind things about me. It's so nice to be praised occasionally. One does try to be of help though heaven knows, there are times when one feels that one wants to give up. I mean, some people are never satisfied, are they? Take the Head for instance. This evening on the staircase he looked at me and sighed. Sighed, I ask you! All right, I may have been tarted up a bit, but only two hours earlier I had helped him to his feet after he had tripped and fallen in the quad. That's the thanks one gets. Oh well, grin and bear it Basil dear. I'm so glad that you have a new job. I imagine it's a sort of promotion, isn't it? How pleased you must be. Heavens, before very long you could be in charge of the whole laundry and not have to put your hands in suds or anything.

Basil

P.S. How sweet of the Snout Baron to give you matchsticks for your house. What a lamb.

St Cloud's

Dear Popsy,

A poem especially for you:

Slopping out is awful
And ping pong's even worse
But Daddy knuckles under
With ne'er a single curse
My daddy is a prisoner
With stripes upon his vest
He helped that poor boy
     Bletchworth
Escape police arrest

They put my daddy in the dock
For all the world to see
Then sent him off to Brixton
A place of misery
His back is bent, his hair is grey
He will not last too long
But Daddy won't die crying
He'll go out with a song!

I do hope you like it. I read it to my navvy and he practically wept. Father Absolute is to read it at Friday's Thanksgiving Service.

Basil

158

Dear Popsy,

Thank you for loving my poem. I wrote it ever so quickly, you know. How I wish you could have been at Thanksgiving Service to hear Father Absolute read it. Everyone was in floods, well almost everyone – Gemini giggled. I'm so glad the Snout Baron likes it. Does he really want me to write one for him? Heavens! Well, I will do my best, but it's going to be awfully difficult – I hardly know the old thing. What have you been up to in the laundry? You haven't been using too much starch again, have you?

Basil

P.S. Maurice Le Vere was attacked and beaten by a Palace customer last night. The attack happened after Maurice forbade the customer to enter Baby's Room during feeding time. Maurice wants the customer banned but Sir Geoffrey thinks we ought to give him another chance.

St Cloud's

Dear Popsy,

Here is the Snout Baron's poem. Tell him that it took me simply ages to write so he'd better think it divine: The Baron of Snout is a perfect dear/My daddy thinks him sweet/He gave my daddy matchsticks/A heavenly little treat/The Baron of Snout has a prisoner boy/A prisoner boy tee hee/He gave the boy five Woodbines/To sit upon his knee/The Baron of Snout is a naughty old trout/He'll have your guts for garters/He'll bite off your nose/Then cut off your toes/And have something else for afters!

I think it's quite a scream don't you?   Basil

St Cloud's

Dear Popsy,

You'll never guess who has written to me . . . the Snout Baron! What a surprise! He says ever such scrumptious things about the poem and you too. He says you have 'class' and 'could go places'. What a dear. He has pasted my poem to his cell wall and reads it each night before lights out. I now have to send him a photograph of myself (he says he has lots of photographs of boys (mainly in swimming shorts!)) which he will paste alongside the poem. He also says that when he gets out he will 'look me up'! I have shown his letter to the Brides and they think it quite the most exciting thing ever.

Basil

P.S. Which photograph of me would the Baron like, do you think? There's one which I had taken at Hastings, but I haven't a stitch on!

St Cloud's

Dear Popsy,

You will have to tell the Snout Baron to be patient. I had planned to send him the Hastings snap but on looking at it I find that my hair is in a state. However, Gemini and I yesterday visited a little photographic studio in town and sat for portraits. I am in profile with my head tilted backwards and my eyes closed. The only other part of my body to be seen is a shoulder (the left one) upon which is perched a largish butterfly made of silk. Gemini is pictured similarly but

160

without the butterfly (he said it looked like a bat). As soon as we receive the copies I will sign one and send it off to the Baron. I will send you one too. How wonderful that you beat Harry the Nose at ping pong.   Basil

St Cloud's

Dear Popsy,

Well, if you will go around hurting people with steam irons you must expect to be punished. Heavens, it was only a silly old ping pong ball that was broken. What would you have done had it been something of value? One shudders to think. I am glad you liked the photographs (my navvy says they make me look proper pretty and has stood one on a shelf in his pigeon loft). Tell the Snout Baron's prisoner boy not to be too jealous. I promise not to steal his Baron away from him! My house tutor has said that I may visit you next week so do try to keep out of trouble. Any more bread and water and there'll be nothing left of you to visit.

                                     Basil

St Cloud's

Dear Popsy,

Sorry, but something has come up which prevents me from visiting you. However, do not despair, you *will* have a visitor – my navvy. He's simply dying to see you. The 'something' which has come up is Courtney Durham's birthday party. I'd quite forgotten it. Will you be too disappointed at not seeing me? I suppose you will be. Oh dear, I do let people down, don't I? I have given my navvy his travelling instructions, but his mind becomes so muddled that he's certain to forget them or mix them up. Do be a dear and make sure he knows which trains he should catch for his return journey. I should hate to lose him!

                                     Basil

Dear Popsy,

My navvy wants me to thank you for being kind to him. He said you were ever so friendly and not a bit put out by his having 'shopped' you. What a peachypoos you are. He also said that you have a broken nose and that you looked 'a proper sight'. Can it be true? Is your nose broken? Oh Popsy, you must stop this fighting. It will only get you into trouble and quite ruin your looks. Guess what happened to my navvy after he left you . . . he boarded the wrong train and finished up in Chipping Norton! Courtney Durham's birthday party was a total bizarrester. The gin ran out, the candles on the cake wouldn't light, and Rory O'Brien had a frightful row with Nipper Thompson after Nipper had called Courtney a greedy bitch for taking the last pickled walnut. Honestly, who'd believe it?!

Basil

P.S. Mother has injured her arm in a climbing accident and will be hors de combat for a month or so. Gemini said it served her right for acting the goat!

Dear Popsy,

It is unimportant that your nose doesn't hurt you; what *is* important is that your nose is broken. Heavens, Popsy, if you carry on like this I'll not be able to recognise you. I'll visit you in prison and a warder or someone will have to point you out to me. 'That's your daddy over there,' he will say, and when I turn around I'll see this awful, ugly man – YOU! I think I'd shriek. I have just started reading *Ruth and Other Tales* by Mrs Gaskell and think it quite fun. Gemini turned his nose up when I told him and said that Mrs Gaskell was a boring old tart. Gemini says that about everyone. I do hope you win your ping pong tournament. Cheery bye.

Basil

P.S. I feel quite shameless tonight!

162

St Cloud's

Dear Popsy,
Your letter mystifies me. Father Absolute is away for a few days visiting his sister and until he returns I cannot get it translated. I have no idea what 'chivved' means, nor do I know the meaning of 'done time for GBH' and 'scarpered when the rozzers moved in and has now got a rub-a-dub in Brighton'. Really, Popsy, I am not one of your prisoner chums, you know. It was wonderful to hear of your ping pong triumph though I do think it unfair that Harry the Nose was nobbled (yes, I do know that word; Nipper Thompson, when he was a jockey, used it all the time). A tempestuous time at the Palace last night. Gemini and I danced to a bit of Borodin and quite drove the customers wild. When we'd finished my judge carried me straight to the rack!

Basil

St Cloud's

Dear Popsy,
Here is a true story: One day last week Basil said to himself he said, 'I know what I'll do – I'll give my daddy a treat. I'll pop down to Brixton and pay him a surprise visit. What fun!' So early the next morning Basil put on his finest clothes, caught the train to London and without stopping for the tiniest bite to eat hurried in the teeming rain to his daddy's prison. But what was Basil told when he arrived there all soaking and sopping wet? I'll tell you what he was told. He was told that he couldn't see his daddy because his daddy had been naughty and was in a punishment cell. I COULD SCREAM!

Basil

St Cloud's

Dear Popsy,
Sorry? I should jolly well hope that you are. You've no idea what I went through. That rain! My hair! I must have

looked like something the cat coughed up. If there's one thing I hate it's to be all wet and squelchy-welchy. How those poor lifeboatmen stand it I'll never know. No, I will not be able to visit you next week, I've much too much to do. Anyway, what would be the point of it? You'd only have been in trouble again and locked away somewhere. Honestly, if you don't mend your ways you'll never get out. Or is that what you want – never to get out, I mean? Gemini and I are thinking of taking ballet lessons. It was my idea. I should so love to be able to leap properly. Borodin's bits were made for leaping to, don't you think? My navvy sends his regards.

Basil

St Cloud's

Dear Popsy,

How proud of you I am. The ping pong champion of Brixton! And in straight sets too! You must be awfully good at it. Did you win a prize – a little cup, perhaps? I'd adore to win a cup – not a huge one, just a little thing that I could dust now and then. I'm being hanged at the Palace tonight and I'm not a bit looking forward to it. I think it must be the weather.

Basil

St Cloud's

Dear Popsy,

And how is my precious animal today? Have you been behaving yourself? Oo, you fibber you. I'll bet you've been fighting like anything. Biff, bang, bang, biff. It's a miracle you're not in bits. I've told Mother about your fighting and she says she always knew you'd turn out a thug, and that if she had wanted a pugilist for a husband she would have married Black Butcher Johnson. Gemini and I visited Courtney Durham's seaside cottage on Saturday and had a heavenly time in the sands and things. I do so love the sea, don't you? I hate the rain, but I love the sea, isn't that odd?

Basil

164

St Cloud's

Dear Popsy,

It's adorable of you to worry about me, but you shouldn't. Everything is simply scrumptious. I have heaps of money, I have my friends, and I have a new colour – turquoise. IT'S ME! From now on everything is to be turquoise. I could EAT IT! But what of you? Are *you* happy? I know that you have told me that you are, but were you just pretending for my sake? If I could only bring some turquoise into your cell – you'd be happy then, I know you would. I had a tiff with my navvy tonight. He wanted to go greyhound racing and when I said no, I'd rather go for a stroll, he started calling me these beastly names. Well, in the end I simply hurled my *Soap and Home* at him and walked off. I'd do anything for him – but greyhound racing! Gemini has a chill, poor luv, and has been shivering and sneezing the whole day. I keep telling him that he should wear something during his Palace rest periods but he won't listen.   Basil

St Cloud's

Dear Popsy,

I will visit you next week. Do, please, stay out of trouble.

Basil

P.S. I have bought you a turquoise scarf which I have sent with a note to the governor asking that it (the scarf) be passed on to you. Have you received it yet? It would look stunning with orange.

P.P.S. Three first years were each given 100 lines today for playing shove ha'penny with their Miraculous Medals!

St Cloud's

Dear Popsy,

Your face was with me from the time I left you to the time I arrived at St Cloud's. It is with me still. When I close my eyes I see it – battered and broken. Oh Popsy, forgive me for having gasped. I kept telling myself all the way to Brixton, 'No matter how awful he looks, Basil, you must not scream or gasp,' but when I saw you. . .! It was like (I have to say it) going to bed with Dr Jekyll and waking up with Mr Hyde. However, you are as you are and we must learn to live with it. As my navvy says, 'It ain't what a bloke looks like what counts, it's what's inside 'im.'   Basil

Dear Popsy,
    It's heaven to know that my visit cheered you. If only the prison were nearer so that I might visit you more often. How much better had you been found insane. You would then have been sent to Longmoor and I could have been popping in and out all the time. Yes, I have 'sprung up' haven't I. I'm almost as tall as Gemini, and Gemini says he's exactly the right height (one more inch he says and the high heels would have to go!). My navvy took me greyhound racing last night and I must say, I quite enjoyed myself. The crowds! I've never been so pressed up against! My navvy won £5 and I won £2. My navvy would have won more but I persuaded him to bet on a dog called Daddy's Precious which lost. The dog he wanted to bet on came first! The look I got! I'm so glad you're getting on well with the new steam irons.   Basil

Dear Popsy,
    I have read of the riot and think it too exciting for words. Are you now getting better food? Father Absolute thinks you should have done as those convicts in America did – held the governor hostage. Next time, perhaps. The newspapers reported that one of the rioters was injured. It wasn't you was it? Please be careful. Riots are divine but they can be dangerous.
                              Basil
P.S. We had a little riot at the Palace on Sunday. Nipper Thompson accused a customer of stealing the rattles from Baby's Room and the customer threw a glass of gin at him. Nipper went quite wild.
P.P.S. Louisa Fryman has a new perfume called Moan. It's heaven.

St Cloud's

Dear Popsy,

That poor prisoner boy. What a beastly thing to have happened. I'll bet the Snout Baron is ever so heartbroken, isn't he? Was the boy the Baron's only boy, or does he have others? Father Absolute thinks he may have as many as half a dozen! It is wonderful to know that your food has improved and that you enjoyed your kippers. My navvy adores kippers and sometimes quite reeks of them. Will the boy have a prison burial or will he be sent home to his mumsy? It's all too sad. Do tell the Baron that he is in my thoughts and that if I could I would hurtle to him.

Basil

P.S. I have bought a recording of Berlioz's Requiem which I adore and which I play over and over. Gemini doesn't like it. He says it's practically impossible to dance to!

St Cloud's

Dear Popsy,

Tingling news! Mother ascends (the Matterhorn) on the 18th! Yes, at last! Isn't it screamy! I shall be there to wave toodle-oo to her (the Head has given me a fortnight off, the luv) so the next time you hear from me I'll be up to my armpits in Alps! Mother is too excited and says she thinks of nothing but crevasses! What clothes should I take with me? Mother is planning victory parties, but one little slip. . . Something in turquoise, I think, and a scrap of black – just to be on the safe side. I will write to you as soon as I arrive. Are you still having kippers for breakfast? Do be careful of those bones.

Basil

P.S. Sir Geoffrey is awfully concerned that my absence from the Palace will upset the Pain Room customers and is pleading with Father Absolute to stand in for me. Father A says he will be put to the rack only if Sir Geoffrey promises a Jesse Window for Holy Room!

Monte Rosa Hotel

Dear Popsy,

    I am here and having a scrumptious time. The place is simply teeming with journalists (Mother calls them the press boys) who follow us everywhere – even in the slush. This morning I met Mother's climbing instructor – a huge thing with a beard that has icicles hanging from it (imagine being kissed by him!). Tomorrow I go in a cable carriage (help!) to the Schwarzsee – a place quite high up and perfect, so I am told, for glacier watching. How I wish you could escape for a day or two and be here with me.

Basil

Monte Rosa Hotel

Dear Popsy,

    Mother and her party set off at 6 a.m. this morning to much pomp and prayer. First a priest from St Bernard's Abbey recited the Glorious Mysteries (Gemini calls them the Glamorous Mysteries!) then, after a speech from the Obermeister in which he recalled poor Mr Whymper's expedition, the town band played a medley from The Maid of the Mountains. It was all too gruesome. Mother told me that if anything happened to her I should try to be brave about it and not make a fuss. (I don't know how I kept a straight face!) The party is expected to reach base camp at 6 p.m. tonight – the time that I have arranged to meet the band's trombone player for drinks!

Basil

P.S. 2 p.m.: I have just had a peek through a huge telescope which has been set up on a balcony so that guests can follow the climbers' progress. Mother looks quite puffed, poor thing. I'm so glad I brought the black!

Monte Rosa Hotel

Dear Popsy,

    I am sure you will already have heard of mother's triumph. She and her party returned at midday today to loud hurrahs and the firing of guns (I was having a perm at the time and thought a revolution had started!). Everyone has gone quite wild with delight. The streets are hung with bunting and a huge crowd is gathered outside the hotel calling for a glimpse of Mother. It's all too frantic. Mother made the most frightful show of herself at the press conference. Not only did she criticise the Swiss for keeping untidy mountains (she said there were enough old bones on the Matterhorn to start a soap factory) but she actually agreed to be photographed waving her false leg. (One photographer wanted her to kiss it!) You've no idea how hideously embarrassed I was. Tonight there is to be a huge party with fireworks and things, but I just want to get away from this beastly place. I WANT MY RACK!

Basil

St Cloud's

Dear Popsy,

Back again and as happy as can be. It's so good to be with one's chums. My return was too wonderful – the whole school turned out and cheered me till my young ears rang. Anyone would have thought that it was I who had trod the peaks! The Head simply gushed about Mother – how brave she was and what a credit she is to the country and all that sort of thing. Honestly, the fuss. It quite made me sick. I'm sure anyone could climb the silly old Matterhorn. The newspapers, of course, are full of it — Mother's climb, I mean. I read in one that she now plans to do the Dolomites. Heaven help them! It was wonderful to have two of your letters waiting for me when I returned. I enjoyed the first, but not the second – all that stuff about your beastly boils. I don't like reading about boils, Popsy. Tonight I am at the Palace and on my rack again. How I've missed it!

Basil

St Cloud's

Dear Popsy,

Here's something to make you die. Last night one of my Palace customers wanted to lash me with a lump of tripe. I told him we didn't keep tripe and suggested a nice bit of rump. No, no, no. He didn't want rump nor did he want belly of pork. It had to be tripe. Honestly, what a performance. In the end Sir Geoffrey had to get his cook to go five miles to her brother's house and pick up a strip from him.

Basil

Dear Popsy,

I would have thought the reason for my not having written to you was obvious. Your last letter quite broke my heart. It broke my heart and made me ill for three days. I could not attend my lessons nor could I attend the Palace. All I kept thinking about was your ear, or what is left of it, and how hideous you must look. Your crushed nose is bad enough, but heavens, one ear! I cannot write more. I feel quite hysterical.

Basil

P.S. I hope the beast who bit it off choked on it.
P.P.S. I have just been sick.

Dear Popsy,

I will continue to write to you only if you promise not to become involved in any more fighting. As for your not being responsible for the last incident, I don't wish to hear about that. All I know is that one doesn't get one's ear bitten off for nothing. If you do not care about yourself then think of me; I'm the one who will have to look at you. Do you still have the ear or has it been thrown away? If you still have it then it may not be too late to have it sewn back on. Do make enquiries.

Basil

P.S. Gemini wants to know if you can paint sunflowers but I don't think it a bit funny.

Dear Popsy,

Of course I forgive you. You are my Popsy and a kinder one never lived. However, you have made me a promise and I expect you to keep it. Now, here is what I have done. I have written to Mr Oosterthing asking him to make you a false ear. (Well, we can't have you semi-eared for the rest of your life, can we?) Mr O will no doubt want to know the size and shape, etc., so what you must do is to get someone to make a life-size drawing of your remaining ear. Do make sure that the drawing

171

is as accurate as possible (use a tape measure) otherwise you might finish up with one lobe longer than the other. Please act quickly.

Basil

P.S. Mr Oosterthing will probably require a drawing of what is left of your bitten-off ear (this for attachment purposes) so put the artist to work on that too. Ugh!

St Cloud's

Dear Popsy,

What big ears you have (had!). I have sent the drawings (Gemini says Leonardo couldn't have done better) to Mr Oosterthing who is awfully keen to get started. He suggests something in rubber – bakelite, he thinks, would be too brittle and might chip or crack if dropped or stepped upon. Also, rubber will allow fingering and bending during moments of concentration (you're always touching an ear, you are, especially when reading. It sometimes drives me mad). Mr O asks if you would like a hair or two (there is no indication of hairs in the drawings) and, if so, what colour? Tawny would be nice, I think, don't you? I have asked Mr O to complete the work as quickly as possible, but do not expect an early delivery – moulds will have to be made and they take time.

Basil

P.S. Mr Oosterthing says Mother is taking a great interest in your 'case' and will personally oversee the work.
P.P.S. My navvy says he once knew a man who had his nose bitten off. I suppose we should think ourselves lucky.

St Cloud's

Dear Popsy,

Don't be a goose – you have not put anyone to the slightest trouble. Heavens, if we can't help out with an ear now and then we might as well cut our wrists. I have changed my mind about the hairs. I now think silver would be better (we all have to face up to our age sooner or later) and have advised Mr Oosterthing so. You surprise me when you say you'd be quite happy with bakelite. You obviously haven't given the matter much thought. Have you never heard the sound of fingernail on bakelite? Tak, tak, tak. I couldn't stand it. The ear must be rubber. Mother writes that she has been invited by the All-England Explorers' Club to give a series of talks on her climb. She arrives in a fortnight and plans to visit you. She hopes to bring the ear with her.   Basil

St Cloud's

Dear Popsy,
    I have a stomach upset and am not feeling at all well. Today has been one long moan and last night at the Palace I was so ill that I had to refuse a triping. Gemini is a dear and keeps me alive with hot milk and honey. How sweet of the Snout Baron to have helped with your bandages. What would we do without our chums? Mother is quite driving me mad with her letters about your ear (the imitation one). It's all too odd. I mean, she never took this interest in you when you were complete, did she? I am feeling ill again so I will end with a little moan.   Basil

St Cloud's

Dear Popsy,
    Thank you, I am much better. Mother arrived yesterday and I am to meet her on Saturday for lunch. She says she will bring the ears (yes, EARS!) with her so that I might see for myself how splendid they are. I'm sure they're perfect little miracles, but heavens, to have them shown to one at lunch is simply too much. I'll cringe, I know I will. How wonderful of the governor to have said what he said. Just think, in two months you could be free! Do, do, do behave yourself.
            Basil
P.S. Mother writes of a Spanish amputee who saved his daughter from drowning by throwing his Limbrub Stroller to her. Mother says that if she had her way *everyone* would be fitted with a Stroller!

St Cloud's

Dear Popsy,

Your ears are darling dears – too lifelike for words. You'll adore them. There are three – two with hairs (silver) and one without. Each ear differs ever so slightly in shape (this to ensure that from one at least you will get a perfect fit) and in colour – pink, pinker and pinkiest. I prefer the pinkiest (it will look divine with your grey tie). Mother has been given special permission by the governor to visit you in his office on the 18th. She will try the ears on you there. Oh Popsy, you'll simply love them. Mr Oosterthing has quite excelled himself. He's even provided a little leather case for the darlings with your name printed inside on a plum velvet lining.

Basil

St Cloud's

Dear Popsy,

I am glad you enjoyed Mother's visit. How wonderful to know that she was kind and sweet to you. It's all too touching. Well, as far as I am concerned Mother is a ghoul – yes, a G-H-O-U-L. Study the facts, do. A few months ago, Mother hated you like anything – she simply loathed the sight of you. Now, all of a sudden, she is attentive and affectionate. Why? BECAUSE YOU HAVE AN ARTIFICIAL EAR, THAT'S WHY. Popsy, Mother's affection is not for you, it is for your ear. HER PASSION IS SURGICAL PARTS! It's all too scary. When I had lunch with her on Saturday, a man with one arm sat down at the table next to ours. Mother stopped eating, looked at him for at least 10 seconds, then turned to me and said, 'What I couldn't do with that fellow'! Macabre wasn't the word!

Basil

Dear Popsy,

You seem to have missed the point I was trying to make. Of course it is better to be shown *any* kind of affection than to be shown none at all. Of course it is commendable to show affection to those who are not entirely whole. But Mother's affection is for artificial limbs, not for the poor luvs who wear them. Mother worships artificial limbs as other women worship pretty jewellery. The amputee means nothing to her – merely a piece of display apparatus upon which to hang a false arm or EAR (her 'jewellery'!). It's too grisly but true. Should you allow yourself to be deceived into thinking that Mother is genuinely fond of you, you will become the display apparatus and your ear a tiara. Do you understand?

Basil

P.S. I found a pig's trotter on the Palace lawn this morning.

Dear Popsy,

Perhaps you are right and I am wrong. Perhaps your ear loss has renewed Mother's fondness for you, but that is no longer important. What now concerns me is that Mother seems to think that when you are released from prison you will return with her to Switzerland and live with her there. I have told her that you would never dream of living in silly old Switzerland. You wouldn't would you, Popsy – live in Switzerland, I mean. I couldn't bear it if you were to leave me here all alone. Please tell Boysie that you won't abandon him.

Basil

P.S. I love your ear just as much as Mother does.

Dear Popsy,

Then go to Switzerland – see if I care. Go and live in the slush with Our Lady of the Alps. I hope you both fall down a crevasse. I hope your beastly ear freezes to bits.

Basil

175

St Cloud's

Dear Popsy,

You bargain with me like a fishwife. Very well – six months in England and six months in Switzerland. I agree to your terms only to make you happy, not because I think them fair or anything like that. I am the one who is being fair, not you. As for the gift you and Mother wish to buy me, let it be Louisa Fryman's Beauty Unlimited (in leather case) price 25 guineas from Harrods.

Basil

P.S. I would prefer it if you were to be in England from April to September.

St Cloud's

Dear Popsy,

A cricket bat! You can tell Mother that if I don't get Beauty Unlimited I will never speak to either of you again.

Basil

St Cloud's

Dear Popsy,

Since I have not heard from you for more than three weeks I must assume that I am not to get Beauty Unlimited. If that is the case then faugh to you and faugh to Mother. You can keep your gifts. With the money I earn at the Palace I can easily afford to buy anything I want. You may not know it but I've got heaps. I could buy a hundred Beauty Unlimiteds if I wanted to.

Basil

St Cloud's

Dear Popsy,

Beauty Unlimited to hand (and eyes, and cheeks, and everywhere!) Oh, it's too gorgeous for words – so many bottles and pots of stuff. It even has a cream which enlarges things!

Basil

P.S. Mother's covering note was beastly, but who cares. She can think whatever she likes of me.

176

St Cloud's

Dear Popsy,

Mother won't be the only one waiting for you at the prison gates. I too will be there – with my navvy – and I'll be tarted up something rotten. Let's see how the old dollop likes that.   Basil

St Cloud's

Dear Popsy,

I am sorry that we parted as we did, but you must blame Mother. Before your arrival she had pulled my navvy's hair and had told him to take his filthy hands off me. She had also slapped my face and had tried to rub off the little something that I had on around my eyes and mouth (didn't you notice how smeared I looked?). Anyway, that's why I was in such a mood. I simply loathe Mother and one of these days I will tell her so to her face. Thank you for being so kind to my navvy. I nearly wept when you took his hand. He adores you but thinks Mother 'a proper old cow'. How right he is. Are you enjoying your freedom? Try not to do too much otherwise you will tire yourself.

Basil

P.S. I thought your ear looked divine, though you might have washed it before you put it on. It was awfully grubby, you know.

St Cloud's

Dear Popsy,

Thank you for your visit. What a heavenly surprise it was. What a glorious day we had. What I most enjoyed was our walk along the river's edge and our jokes about things. How loudly we laughed. We must have quite terrified the little fishes! I was awfully late at the Palace. Sir Geoffrey was frightfully peeved and practically threw me into the Pain Room! Tonight I am going greyhound racing with my navvy and Father Absolute. Father A says there is a dog running in

177

the third race which is a 'cert'. He is going to put a 'fiver' on it and advises me to do the same. Isn't he a lark.

Basil

P.S. The Head wanted to know who my 'brutish-looking' friend was. He meant you!

St Cloud's

Dear Popsy,

Your letter was a joy and cheered me up no end. I loved the bit about Aunt Amethyst and what she asked Mother about bedtimes. How naughty of her. When I told Gemini he simply screamed and said that if you and Mother were to embrace too passionately you'd both come apart! Now for some sad news. My navvy's mother has been taken ill and is not expected to last out the week. It seems she has a ruined liver (she drinks gin like anything) and a faulty heart. My navvy is awfully upset, poor luv, and was practically in tears last night. 'I'll miss that old ratbag,' he said. 'I'll miss her good and proper.' It's all too sad. Tonight we visit her in hospital.

Basil

St Cloud's

Dear Popsy,

My navvy's mother died at 10 a.m. yesterday. My navvy was with her at The End. Her last words (the first in two years!) were, 'Don't forget to put the cat out'! My navvy is quite distraught, poor luv, and drinks and weeps all over the place. Today he asked Courtney Durham if he might 'stow the old lady' with Mrs D in her elephant tomb, to save him 'a few bob' on funeral costs. Courtney has agreed (he said my navvy could put whatever he liked in there!) and has even offered to arrange for his stonemason to inscribe a few words on one of the elephant's ears. I think it's ever so kind of him, don't you?

Basil

St Cloud's

Dear Popsy,

I have passed on your words to my navvy who thanks you and says you are a saint. I wasn't able to attend the funeral (the Head asked me what my relationship was to the deceased and when I told him that she was the mother of a friend he said that if the friend was that loathsome old man he had seen me with then he would have to refuse permission) but my navvy says the whole thing went off quite beautifully. There wasn't a dry eye in the church and everyone got 'proper pickled'. I am glad that you are happier now than you have ever been and that Mother is 'sweet' to you. Perhaps I should have an ear bitten off and she might be sweet to me. However, do continue to enjoy yourself, and think of me occasionally.

Basil

St Cloud's

Dear Popsy,

Your letter quite shook me. Why couldn't you have *told* me that you were going to Switzerland? You're getting as bad as Mother, you are – dashing off without so much as a cheerio. I could never have done such a thing to you — not in a million years. Heavens, Popsy, all I ask is a little consideration. Perhaps I expect too much. Anyway, you are back and glad to be so, I'll be bound. Switzerland is such an old yawn, isn't it? – and so lumpy. What a scream that everyone thinks you a thug. Personally I rather like cruel-looking men (how I'd love to have met Geronimo!). Do write soon and swear on your sacred word of honour that you will never again dash off without first telling your

Kiddie

P.S. If you think your life hectic, what of mine? Last night at the Palace I was stretched, hanged and triped!

179

Dear Popsy,

It was not necessary to send me money (I have heaps) but thank you just the same. I bought a little something for my legs with it. How wonderful that the false hand is now ready for production. Where *does* Mr Oosterthing get his patience from? I'd have given up with that finger ages ago. Can it do anything else apart from beckon, do you know? It would be too heavenly if it could waggle or something. I am not sure that I like The Gripper as a name – what about Handyhand or Hold Tight? The Gripper sounds much too scary. Yes, it certainly is strange that so many of our relatives have been robbed of late but I do not know that you should suspect the Snout Baron. Just because he wanted a few addresses does not make him a criminal. He'd be awfully upset to know that you distrusted him. Anyway, Aunt Amethyst and the others deserved to be robbed. They're a lot of old meanies.

Basil

St Cloud's

Dear Popsy,

Finger Prince is adorable – much better than The Gripper. How clever you are. Have you told Mother? I'm sure she'd love it. Mother says the hand is capable of crushing a cocoa tin into a tiny ball. Heavens! Prison quite seems to have made a new man of you. I too am feeling fit though I cannot say that I am enjoying myself. I simply loathe school work – maths and history. Ugh! I got the most frightful ticking off the other day for not knowing the square root of something. Gemini and I are throwing on our rags tonight and popping into town. We won't to anything there, just loiter, and hope that somebody a little barbaric comes along!

Basil

P.S. I have bought an electric carpet sweeper. The suction!

St Cloud's

Dear Popsy,

I am glad all goes well with the Gripper and that Limbrub Ltd continues to prosper. How lucky we are, and thank heaven for Mr Oosterthing. This morning I was at my navvy's cottage helping him sell his mother's clothes. The crowd! Just like Harrods at Christmas. Nipper Thompson bought an old fox thing that smelled of carbolic and had an acid drop stuck to it, and Gemini a round black hat with a lemon ribbon; too gruesome for words. I wouldn't be seen dead in either of them. Mass in half an hour so I'd better start tarting myself up. Cheery bye.

Basil

P.S. GET THAT MUCUS AND CLOGGING CATARRH CLEARED UP WITH DR DODD'S LINCTUS.

St Cloud's

Dear Popsy,

I wrote to Mother yesterday so your wish has been answered. However, I could not write what you wanted me to. I do not feel for Mother what *you* feel, Popsy. I do not love her as you do. I loathe her. I always shall! If you are unhappy with your tiepin then you must take it back and select another – a pretty pearly one perhaps. Pearls, pearls! I dote on them!

There is a tat-a-tat-tak upon my door. It is Gemini; I must dash.

Basil

P.S. Gemini is in feathers tonight!

St Cloud's

Dear Popsy,

How wonderful it is that you are to make the Gripper presentation. How thrilled you must be. Do you know how the dear came to lose his hand? It wasn't while working for Limbrub was it? That would be too awful. Do be gentle with him when you strap it on.

181

I am glad that you are pleased with your new tiepin. Does it sparkle like anything? I do love a bit of sparkle, don't you? – it makes one feel so cheap! Have a safe journey.

Basil

St Cloud's

Dear Popsy,

I have just had a letter from Mother telling of your accident. Really, Popsy, something must be done about the Gripper. It is quite ridiculous that one cannot shake hands with it without having one's bones crushed. (How you must have screamed.) I shall write to Mother suggesting that alterations be carried out to make it less ferocious. We simply cannot allow the public to be exposed to such a danger. Mother says that you are enjoying yourself (in that slush?) and that you are taking a great interest in Limbrub Ltd. She says you've even been helping pack legs.

Anyway, I've decided to let my hair grow. I want it wild and long.

Basil

St Cloud's

Dear Popsy,

I agree with you – it *is* sensible of Mother to have had the Grippers recalled. Let us hope that we are not too late. . .! News of me? There is nothing to tell; I simply soldier on from day to day. Yesterday I went for a stroll with my navvy (he wanted to break in a new pair of boots, bless his heart) and on Wednesday I did a bit of ironing for him. Honestly, since his mother died he's become quite lost. He can't do a thing for himself. You should see his bedroom. The mess!

Something odd at the Palace the other evening; I entered the Pain Room and found a bucket of offal standing by my rack. It was my tripe man's. It's his new 'thing'. Offal though! Thank heaven it had been warmed up! I am glad that your hand is better.

Basil

St Cloud's

Dear Popsy,

How you do go on about Mother. How you sing her praises. Yesterday she was working her fingers to the bone, and today she is clever and loving. What will she be tomorrow – a beauty perhaps? My tripe man has asked me to be his companion. He's awfully rich and says I wouldn't want for anything. I must say the idea of being someone's companion does rather appeal, though I don't know that I could stand a life of tripe (last night I was simply draped in it!) I've told him that he must wait until I'm a little older.

Father Absolute wants to know if you would like any puppet Madonnas. He says he can 'do' you a gross for £50.

Basil

P.S. When I've posted this I'm going to slip into something tropical!

St Cloud's

Dear Popsy,

How it rains. It's simply gushing down and has been for the past three days. Yesterday the dining hall was flooded and everyone was ordered to mop up. Gemini refused saying he wouldn't be seen dead with a bucket, and was given 500 lines. I would like to have done the same (refuse to mop up, I mean) but I didn't have the courage. The result was that I was splashed and everything.

Mother tells me that the Gripper has been hailed as the most exciting artificial limb since the mechanical hook which is heavenly news. It would be wonderful if Mr Oosterthing were to win another Golden Spanner, wouldn't it? Mother says that in a few months the Gripper will be as famous as the Holy Hand of St Edmund!

Basil

St Cloud's

Dear Popsy,

Of course I won't breathe a word about the Gripper business. How ghastly though. That poor baby boy. What a way to go – crushed to bits by his daddy's false hand. Eek! Thank heaven the police are not making a fuss. I mean, if it were ever to get into the newspapers. . . How much compensation is Mother paying? Heaps, I suppose.

Courtney Durham has broken a leg vaulting and is in plaster, poor luv. Rory O'Brien carries him on his back! Nipper Thompson got drunk at the Palace on Sunday and attacked a customer with a feeding bottle. Honestly!

Basil

St Cloud's

Dear Popsy,

How are you? Are you being a good nanny goat? Mother seems to think so. Mother says that you are 'proving a real asset' to Limbrub Ltd and that as a reward you are to have your own office. I'll bet you're ever so pleased about that, aren't you? Mother also says that the Stroller de Luxe is now 'de rigueur' for amputees and that the Gripper looks like setting a new sales record (I never knew that there were that many luvs without hands, did you?). Anyway, Mother says our futures are secure which is scrumptious news.

Gemini is sprawled on my chaise longue looking at his nails. You should see what he's wearing. He'll be lucky if he gets out of the Palace in one bit tonight!

Basil

St Cloud's

Dear Popsy,

What a cheek of Aunt Amethyst turning up uninvited. I would have sent the stinking old slut packing. You're too kind, Popsy, that's your trouble.

I have a new Palace customer who is something big in the Wholesale Co-operative Society. He's awfully sweet and brings me packets of tea and things. He likes to be smacked with a coal shovel!

How lucky Mother is to be going to America. Don't you wish you were going too? I should love to see the Empire State Building and everything, wouldn't you? I sometimes crave for New York, I really do.   Basil

St Cloud's

Dear Popsy,

The first thing I must tell you is that I am in curls! Blame Gemini. He said that if I didn't do something with my hair (it's as long as anything!) I'd be arrested; so out came the tongs! Heaven knows what my house tutor will say when he sees me. He hates me as it is. He sneers at me! My second news is that my navvy has won a prize with one of his pigeons. Isn't that wonderful? He's ever so thrilled, bless him.

Gemini and I played Three Wishes today. Gemini's wishes were to have a huge bosom; to be ravished in the ribbon department at Harrods, and to paint the Taj Mahal black!! Honestly!

I MUST GET SOME CLOTHES!   Basil

                                          St Cloud's
Dear Popsy,

Mother writes from America that she may have found factory premises in 'downtown Manhattan'. Downtown Manhattan, how romantic! Does everyone there play a banjo, do you think? And tapdance? How I'd love to be able to tapdance. Tippety-tap, tappety-tip. Heaven. I have passed on your congratulations to my navvy who thanks you and sends you this feather (I hope it stays stuck) from the winning bird. It's a pretty colour but not, I think, as nice as the feather you brought from the fens.   Basil

                                          St Cloud's
Dear Popsyplums,

A letter from Mother this morning saying that she is to rent the premises in Manhattan, but perhaps you already know this. Oh Popsy, I should so love to go to America and be bad in Manhattan!

I'll bet the Snout Baron was ever so thrilled to get your letter. How it must have warmed his dear heart. That poor luv; it's too awful that he has to be stuck away in that beastly old prison. I wonder if he still has my picture by his bed – or have I been replaced by someone a little bolder, do you think?!!

                                          Basil
P.S. My tripe man hates my curls. He says he wants me boyish – the more boyish the better!

186

St Cloud's

Dear Popsy,

These lines come to you from the Palace on a Sunday evening. It is ever so warm and I am wearing only a scrap of tulle and leg irons – the keys to which have been lost. In a few moments a blacksmith will arrive to chisel me free. Next to me sits Gemini looking at his hands (as usual) and there are happy gurgling noises coming from Baby's Room. It's almost Tolstoy, isn't it?! How odd that the Snout Baron hasn't replied to your letter. Perhaps he's been busy rioting or something. Oh well, you've always got your boysie haven't you?

Basil

St Cloud's

Dear Popsy,

Your letter arrived with one from Mother. Yours was best; Mother's was full of factory news and tales of the Gripper (it seems the Americans are awfully fond of it, bless them, and want more). Has mother told you that she intends staying on in Manhattan? I imagine she has. Yes, of course I will drop Mr Oosterthing a line. I do hope he's feeling better and not in too much pain. In the meantime please give the old luv a squeeze for me. Your new skis sound adorable. Will you be able to go awfully fast on them? Whoosh! Heavens!

The Head took me into a corner of the quad today and asked me if I didn't think my hair was too long. I said that I didn't and he let me go. What a peach.   Basil

St Cloud's

Dear Popsy,

Isn't life too absurd? I have been hanged five times in the last three months (once with a roughish bit of wire) and I never once felt a twinge. Last night I slept with a window open and today I am in agonies from a stiff neck. Honestly! If you miss Mother *that* much why don't you pop over to Manhattan? I'm sure Mr Oosterthing could manage without you. You are mistaken if you think I would enjoy skiing. I have seen people ski and I know how wet they get.   Basil

Dear Popsy,

    Lucky you with your suntan. How you must stand out against the Alps. I'm as white as anything. I'm sure that if I were naked and lost in an avalanche I'd never be found! Yes, my neck is ever so much better which is a mercy because tonight I have three Palace customers and one of them is bound to want to string me up. Last Sunday when the pain was at its worst my noose man had me in a steel collar. I screamed, twice. Gemini has seen your snapshot and says you look like a fairground fighter!

    My hair is awfully free tonight.

Basil

P.S. We seem to have lost Sir Geoffrey. He hasn't been seen for two days and his housekeeper says his bed hasn't been slept in.

St Cloud's

Dear Popsy,

    There is a frightful row going on here and I am in the most awful trouble. It's all to do with a picture that appeared on the front page of Thursday's *Daily Glimmer* which shows me with a Palace customer. I am not recognisable because my face has been blanked out, but my Palace man (he's wearing a dog collar and chain!) is named as the Foreign Secretary! Honestly, I can't believe it – that he's the Foreign Secretary, I mean; he told me he was a dentist! Anyway, yesterday I was questioned for four hours by two men from MI5. They wanted to know simply everything about me and the Palace and said that had I been older I would have been arrested. They also said that Sir Geoffrey Grassington is working for a foreign nation and that it was he who supplied the *Daily Glimmer* with the photograph. It seems he wants to make things beastly for the government. It's all a scream really, I suppose.

Basil

P.S. I am writing a new poem – 'Ta ta to Taffeta'.

St Cloud's

Dear Popsy,

Please don't make a fuss; I've enough fuss-makers here without you too. Since my last card the Palace has been closed (there's a police guard at the door) and there have been other photographs in the *Daily Glimmer* – one of me with the Defence Minister; one of Father Absolute, also with the Defence Minister, and one of Gemini with somebody in a mask and ball gown. The *Glimmer* is saying that it's the First Sea Lord! The whole thing has caused the most ghastly scandal and simply everyone is leaving. Fifteen boys went on Sunday and another two dozen leave this weekend. The Head is absolutely livid and says that as soon as the inquiries are over Gemini and I are to be sacked. He says we've ruined him!

I picked a branch of white blossom today.
Basil

P.S. My MI5 men say that Sir Geoffrey has been spotted in Latvia!

St Cloud's

Dear Popsy,

No, do not come here. If you do, Mother will realise that I am involved. (She has written asking who the boys in the photographs are (the story is in all the American newspapers, apparently) and I have told her that they are two first years. You must say the same). The Head announced this morning that St Cloud's is to close. He looked straight at me and made the most ghastly face. I felt awful and blushed like anything. There are only 20 boys left and he said he could no longer afford to keep the school open. The English prof was in tears!

Did you know that the Foreign Secretary and the Defence Minister have resigned? Isn't it too sad? I do feel sorry for them because they're such luvs. The Defence Minister used to call me his little chum. Heaven knows what I shall do when the school closes. I think I might take up my tripe man's offer and be his companion. Gemini hopes to model for Schiaparelli.
Basil

P.S. My hair is in braids tonight so I'm looking a little Saxon!

St Cloud's

Dear Popsy,

The school closes on Friday 21st and I shall be sailing with my tripe man to North Africa at 12 midnight on the same date. I'm so excited I could leap! North Africa! All those yashmaks and things! Gemini is off to Schiaparelli (she's frightfully keen to have him) and Father Absolute is to write his memoirs for the *Daily Glimmer*. He's being paid heaps, lucky beast. Something too wonderful happened last night – Courtney Durham and Rory O'Brien were married at a secret ceremony in St Agnes the Divine's. Father Absolute officiated and Gemini and Nipper Thompson were bridesmaids. Best man was my navvy (how his boots squeaked!) Anyway, it was heaven, and afterwards – after gallons of gin – Courtney and Rory left for Courtney's seaside cottage where they are to live. It's all too romantic.

Basil

P.S. *The Times* is saying that the Palace scandal is likely to bring down the government. Heavens!

The Gannet
Poole Harbour

Dear Popsy,

Here I am aboard my tripe man's yacht (it's simply huge!) and feeling just a little steerage after a gruesome rail journey. The train was hot and filthy and I haven't yet recovered from it. When I've finished this my tripe man is to hose me down. It was too awful leaving St Cloud's. How I shall miss it. Gemini and I were in floods. We have promised to write once a week and to meet at *least* three times a year. Before we left, the Head gave us the most frightful talking to. He said we were 'vile bits of sewage – corrupt and pagan'! I giggled like anything. Father Absolute and Nipper Thompson are here for a party we are to have before sailing. They're such treasures, I don't know what I shall do without them. Father Absolute is going to open a betting office and will employ Nipper as his runner. Isn't that sweet of him?

190

Well, Popsy, I've simply no idea when you'll next hear from me. Is the N. African post reliable, do you think? Write to me c/o The Gannet. Do try to see my navvy whenever possible. I begged him to come with us but he refuses to leave his pigeons, bless him. He's named one after me; it's auburn and has orange eyes!

Oh dear, my tripe man calls me to the hose. Do take care, and don't think too badly of your kiddie. GOODBYE!

Basil

P.S. Isn't it a scream about the government?